The Methuen Book
of Contemporary
Latin American Plays

La Chunga by Mario Vargas Llosa
Paper Flowers by Egon Wolff
Medea in the Mirror by José Triana

La Chunga: 'La Chunga is the proprietress, sultry, embittered, enigmatic. Every night a gang of four men come to drink her beer, throw dice and trade mild insults. Not surprisingly in such a place, time turns out to be circular rather than linear . . . the subtle, teasing inter-weaving of present and past, reality and fantasy is not gratuitous: it becomes a means of revealing what lies behind the rigid and repeated postures of the sexual game. One by one the men are summoned to the bed chamber-come-confessional . . . Gwynne Edwards' translation of this clever play speaks idiomatically.' _The Times_

Paper Flowers: 'A thrilling discovery . . . sexual and social threat and promise slide in both directions. The atmosphere is half boudoir, half school playground. Chilean playwright Egon Wolff clearly knows and admires his absurdist forebears by this is no knock-off job. The battle between the black comedy of social usurpation and the tragedy of sexual longing is well-balanced and its final slide into nightmare has all the awful pull of a sudden undertow in deep waters.' _Time Out_

'Egon Wolff's play is a powerfully visceral piece of theatre.' _Evening Standard_

The Methuen Book of
Contemporary Latin American Plays

*Translated and
introduced by Gwynne Edwards*

La Chunga
by
Mario Vargas Llosa

Paper Flowers
by
Egon Wolff

Medea in the Mirror
by
José Triana

Methuen Drama

METHUEN CONTEMPORARY DRAMATISTS

Published by Methuen 2004

1 3 5 7 9 10 8 6 4 2

First published in 2004 by
Methuen Publishing Limited,
215 Vauxhall Bridge Road,
London SW1V 1EJ

Methuen Publishing Limited Reg. No. 3543167

A CIP catalogue record for this book is available from the British
Library.

ISBN 0 413 77378 7

Typeset by SX Composing DTP, Rayleigh, Essex
Printed and bound in Great Britain by
Cox and Wyman Ltd, Reading, Berkshire

Contents

Introduction

Latin America, or Spanish America if Portuguese-speaking Brazil is excluded, consists of some twenty different countries and is, in every sense, a continent of enormous fascination. Geographically, it enjoys a diversity which ranges from the great mountain chain of the Andes to the vast pampas of Argentina and the tropical jungles of the Amazon. The rich variety of its ancient native cultures may still be seen, not least in the ruins of Macchu Picchu, while the Spanish heritage of the 'conquistadores' is everywhere evident in the cathedrals, churches, and other buildings of its towns and cities. And in political terms, of course, Latin America has always been a place of huge ferment, ever associated in the foreign imagination with revolutions, military coups, and oppressive dictatorships. It is a context in which, not surprisingly, the arts have flourished. Gabriel Garcia Márquez's *One Hundred Years of Solitude*, and Mario Vargas Llosa's *Aunt Julia and the Scriptwriter* and *The War of the End of the World*, are novels which have achieved worldwide fame, and it is hardly surprising that theatre, a form which so often reflects the social and political climate, should also have flourished in such a rich environment, though it has to be said that Latin American theatre has been a relatively late developer, slow to make its mark on the international stage. All the dramatists represented here have been involved in or responded in one way or another to the political and social events of their particular countries: Mario Vargas Llosa in Peru; José Triana in Cuba; and Egon Wolff in Chile. But although their theatre expresses the issues and concerns of the countries to which they belong, and frequently does so in a language and style which draws on the cultural heritage of those countries, the hallmark of these writers is in the end their ability to transcend the boundaries and limitations of the particular events of a play and to present the problems of men and women in a much broader context.

Prior to the arrival of the Spanish 'conquistadores' in the sixteenth-century, theatre in Latin America had taken the form of native ritualistic spectacles. Subsequently, under the influence of the new arrivals and the Catholic Church, a religious drama flourished, and then a more secular theatre which owed much to the traditions of seventeenth-century Spanish writers. In the eighteenth and nineteenth centuries Latin American theatre continued to be largely influenced by European neoclassical and Romantic models, and it was not until the beginning of the twentieth century that theatrical forms began to emerge which sought to express the continent's vitality and independence. A huge influx of European immigrants into Argentina and Buenos Aires in particular inspired, for example, the so-called urban *sainete*, a theatrical form marked by its emphasis on local colour and realistic language. In addition, the early part of the century saw the emergence of plays in which rural life, embodied in the character of the *gaucho*, was seen to be threatened by increasing urbanisation. A vigorous drama began to develop in relation to issues which were specifically Latin American.

The end of the First World War in 1918 had as profound an effect in Latin American countries as elsewhere, not least with regard to the search for new forms of theatrical expression. Influenced by the European avant-garde, new experimental groups began to appear, such as Teatro de Ulises in Mexico in 1928, and Teatro de la Cueva in Cuba, all of them rejecting outdated forms of theatre, developing new spaces, and seeking innovative styles of acting and design. Furthermore, if these new ideas were at first applied to the work of European dramatists in translation, it was not long before Latin American dramatists attempted to break away from that tradition. In Mexico Efrén Orozco Rosales wrote plays of a strongly nationalist character, of which *Liberation* (*Liberación*, 1929) is one example, while in Argentina Roberto Arlt produced a body of work in the 1930s in which the mixture of reality and fantasy anticipates the theatre of later writers, not least Mario Vargas Llosa. During the same decade Puerto Rican travelling theatre groups performed a *commedia dell'arte* kind of theatre which focused on local issues and types, underlining the way in which there, as elsewhere, dramatists were beginning to be concerned with problems relevant to the Latin American experience.

Between 1940 and 1960 the trend described above acquired added impetus. 1941 saw the opening of the Cuban Academia de las Artes Dramáticas, and 1949 the inauguration in Havana of the Teatro Experimental, whose function it was to develop national playwrights. The same period witnessed the setting up of the Compañía Nacional de Comedias and the Escuela Nacional de Arte Escénica in Peru, and in Mexico the Instituto Nacional de Bellas Artes. In the light of such developments, it was inevitable that new dramatists should emerge. In Mexico, Rodolfo Usigli, an admirer of European theatre and especially of George Bernard Shaw, wrote plays which satirised contemporary political life and revealed the tensions within middle-class families. The Argentinian dramatist, Osvaldo Dragún, exposed the corruption of the political system and was constantly concerned with the question of social injustice. In Cuba, Virgilio Piñera, an important influence on José Triana, employed black humour to expose the reality behind the façade of national happiness, and in Peru, Sebastián Salazar Bondy, experimenting in a variety of theatrical forms, achieved international status.

The most productive period in Latin American theatre has, however, been the last forty years. The 1960s and 70s saw political upheavals in many countries: in Cuba the revolution of 1959; in Argentina the military coup which initially overthrew Perón, and in 1976 the advent of another military dictatorship; in Chile the overthrow in 1973 of the left wing government led by Salvador Allende and the beginning of the notorious military dictatorship of Augusto Pinochet. Quite clearly, events of this kind were bound to stimulate theatrical activity in one way or another. The work of the Argentinian dramatist, Griselda Gambaro, revealed the violence that had and would characterise the various military regimes and led to her exile to Spain in 1976. Between 1960 and 1980 there emerged the New Theatre, initially championed in Colombia by Enrique Buenaventura's Teatro Experimental de Cali. Its purpose was to provide an alternative to bourgeois theatre, rejecting in the process the notion of an individual author, encouraging collective work in relation to all aspects of performance, and inviting audience participation. The devised play flourished in this environment and was enthusiastically taken up in other Latin American countries, notably in Cuba and in the work of the Brazilian and Nicaraguan dramatists, Augusto Boal and Alan Bolt. On the other hand, collective theatre has been criticised by many writers who consider that, precisely because of its emphasis on group participation and non-textual elements, it diminishes the importance of the spoken word and the individual dramatist.

Since the 1980s military dictatorships have, with the exception of Cuba, given way to largely democratic regimes, even though the Peruvian example of recent years (see later) suggests that old political habits die hard. This general shift of political emphasis has meant, in consequence, that the concerns of dramatists have moved from the political and the social to the personal, and that in many cases writers have become more interested in such matters as sexuality, gender and identity, and the power of the imagination.

For all the variety and richness of Latin American culture and history, theatre in this great continent has always had its problems. The commercial theatre exists even today only in the large cities such as Buenos Aires and Mexico City, and even there on a smaller scale than in London and other major European cities. Runs also tend to be short, which means that dramatists can earn more and be more secure either by writing for television or by moving to other countries. Nevertheless, Latin America has produced playwrights of outstanding talent, as the plays included in this collection suggest.

Mario Vargas Llosa

Mario Vargas Llosa was born in 1936 in the town of Arequipa in southern Peru. Before Mario's birth his father had abandoned his wife, but he returned to the family home more than ten years later. Observing the extent to which his young son was already devoted to literature, he sent him to the Leoncio Prada military academy in the capital, Lima, in the hope that the experience would make a man of him and rid him of what his father regarded as a pointless and effeminate activity. Hating the kind of life he encountered there, Mario subsequently studied literature and law at the University of San Marcos in Lima, and in 1955, when he was nineteen, eloped with his aunt, Julia Urquidi, thirteen years his senior, whom he divorced in 1964. In the late 1950s he began a sixteen-year period of self-imposed exile, dividing his time between Madrid, London and Paris, where in 1965 he married his cousin, Patricia. In 1974 he set up home once more in Lima and from that time became more directly involved in the politics of his homeland, to the point where, in 1987, his disillusionment with Peruvian politics led him to run for president. Standing on a conservative platform which he considered best suited to deal with the political and economic instability of Peru, he was defeated in the 1990 elections by Alberto Fujimori, the son of Japanese immigrant parents. Elected for a second term in 1995, Fujimori, whose periods in office had become increasingly authoritarian, was forced to stand down in 2000 over charges of corruption. Even so, Vargas Llosa's failure to win the presidency ten years earlier has been seen by many to have been his salvation as a writer.

Vargas Llosa's enormous success as a novelist has been as great as that of any Latin American writer. To date he has written thirteen novels which have been translated into many languages and which include titles as familiar as *The Time of the Hero* (1963), *Aunt Julia and the Scriptwriter* (1977), *The War of the End of the World* (1981), *In Praise of the Stepmother* (1988), *Death in the Andes* (1993), *The Notebooks of Don Rigoberto* (1997), and, more recently, *The Feast of the Goat*. As far as

theatre is concerned, he has written five plays, beginning in
1981 with *The Young Lady from Tacna*, and following it with
Kathie and the Hippopotamus in 1983, *La Chunga* in 1986, *The
Madman of the Balconies* in 1993, and *Nice Eyes, Ugly Paintings*
in 1996. They reflect an interest in writing for the theatre
which, in different circumstances, might have led to his
becoming a full-time dramatist, as he has himself observed:

> If in Lima in the 1950s, where I began writing, there had
> existed a theatre movement, it is probable that I would
> have become a playwright rather than a novelist. The
> theatre was my first love, ever since, in short trousers, I
> saw a performance of Arthur Miller's *Death of a Salesman*
> by the Argentinian company of Francisco Petrone. But to
> write plays in the Lima of that time was worse than
> weeping: it was virtually to condemn oneself to never
> seeing one's work staged, something even sadder and
> more frustrating than for a poet or a novelist to die
> without his work being published.
>
> Although I have devoted my life to other genres, my
> early love for the theatre never disappeared completely. It
> continued to beat there in the background, showing signs
> of life every few years, as the plays in this collection prove.
>
> To write them was always a pleasure, and always a
> lesson in modesty and synthesis, for unlike the all-
> powerful and free novelist, the dramatist has to accept his
> status as a mere cog in a machine in which actors,
> directors, stage designers, and time and the media too,
> play a vital part in the success or failure of the show.

Vargas Llosa's fascination with theatre stems largely from
his preoccupation with the need and capacity of human
beings to create for themselves a world of fantasy and
illusion, which is what theatre itself often is in relation to its
audience. In *Kathie and the Hippopotamus*, for example, Kathie
Kennety, a wealthy and mature widow, hires a journalist
and lecturer, Santiago Zavala, to help her transform her
story of her travels into the kind of colourful and exotic
account she is herself incapable of writing. For Kathie the

experience is an escape from the monotony of her everyday life, for Santiago a compensation for his not possessing the literary gifts of his idol, Victor Hugo. In the course of the exercise, moreover, the story dictated by Kathie and embroidered by Santiago becomes interwoven with events from their respective pasts – their marriages, his affair with a student – in which they act out the parts, reality and fiction intertwined and coloured by memory, fantasy and desire. In his introductory comments to the text of the play Vargas Llosa has stated the matter very clearly:

> To lie is to invent; to add to real life a fictitious element which passes for reality . . . Fiction is the life that was not, the life we would like to have had but did not . . . Thanks to the conceits of fiction, we can expand our experience of life – a man can become many other men, a coward a brave man, a virgin a prostitute . . . The lie of fiction enriches our existence . . .
>
> Theatre is not life, but make-believe, which is to say another life, a life of fiction, of lies. No genre presents as wonderfully as theatre does the equivocal character of art. The characters we observe on stage, unlike those we encounter in novels or paintings, are flesh and blood, acting out their roles before our very eyes. If the performance is successful, we are convinced of their authenticity by the way they speak, move, gesture and reveal their emotions. Are we conscious that there is a difference between them and real life? No, we are not, other than that we know they are a pretence, a fiction, that they are theatre . . . The role of theatre – of fiction in general – is to create an illusion, to deceive . . .
>
> Dreaming, writing works of fiction (no less than reading, seeing plays, suspending belief) is an oblique way of making a stand against the mediocrity of life . . . Fiction . . . makes us feel complete, . . . and when it restores us once more to our normal condition, we realise that we have changed, that we are more conscious of our limitations, more eager for fantasy and less willing to accept the status quo . . .

The setting and the social status of the characters in *La Chunga* are very different from those of *Kathie and the Hippopotamus*. The action takes place in the outskirts of Piura, the city where Vargas Llosa spent part of his childhood. In this run-down neighbourhood, La Chunga, a strong-willed, tough and ageless woman, runs a bar in which four men – El Mono, José, Josefino and Lituma – meet each night to drink and play dice. Some time ago Josefino had arrived with his latest girlfriend, the young and attractive Meche, whom he had loaned to La Chunga in exchange for money he needed to continue playing. Since that night nothing more has been heard of Meche, and now, many months later, the four men begin to wonder what might have occurred, each of them in turn fantasising about his relationship with Meche, or with Meche and La Chunga, or indeed with La Chunga herself.

As this summary suggests, the theme of fantasy and illusion is as central to *La Chunga*, despite its different mileau, as it is to *Kathie and the Hippopotamus*. Furthermore, Vargas Llosa has emphasised that the fantasies of the characters are as much a part of them as the reality of their daily lives:

> The characters of the play are simultaneously themselves and their fantasies, people of flesh and blood whose destinies are conditioned by particular limitations – they are poor, uneducated, on the fringes of society – but they are also spirits for whom, despite the harshness and monotony of their lives, there is always the possibility of relative freedom, which is the province of imagination, that human attribute par excellence . . .

This said, the male characters are seen to be very different in their fantasies from the image they give to others in their daily lives. In the card game, for example, El Mono brags, boasts, presents himself as one of the lads. In his fantasy, on the other hand, he emerges as a person racked by guilt, confessing to having raped a little girl when he was younger and accepting a beating for it. José and Lituma, similarly outgoing and aggressive in their public behaviour, are in the private world of their dreams the very opposite: José a man who, rather than make love to women, likes to imagine women making love to each other; Lituma a gentle romantic soul who imagines himself running off with Meche. The explanation for this fundamental difference between the public and the private persona of these individuals lies in the fact that in Latin America, as in Spain and other Mediterranean countries, a man's honour is of prime importance, which means in effect that, in their dealings with other men in particular, El Mono, José, and Lituma are obliged to conceal their real natures behind a façade of virility and manliness. Queers, voyeurs and paedophiles cannot afford to admit to their true natures in a world in which the womanising, strutting Josefino sets the standard. As well as this, *La Chunga* also reveals, of course, the inferior position of women in a world in which men like Josefino rule the roost, considering women as little more than sexual objects to be displayed and exploited in the interests of male vanity and pleasure. It is significant that in his own fantasy Josefino imagines himself to be even more macho than he is in reality.

As the above suggests, *La Chunga* is a play of considerable achievement in terms of characterisation. The four male characters are sharply drawn and strongly differentiated, particularly in the course of their fantasies, and, despite their moral weaknesses, frequently arouse our sympathy. Of the women, Meche is young and naïve, not especially deep, but La Chunga is a constant source of fascination, hardened by her experience, mysterious in her silences, as much an enigma to her customers as to ourselves in the sense that little is revealed about her past. She is, indeed, a character with whom, although she is rooted in Piura, we can all identify and understand, as is the case with the four men, who, escaping from the monotony of their lives into a world of dream, could exist anywhere. And finally, *La Chunga* has a complex and fascinating structure, its frequent shifts between reality and fantasy filling out before our eyes the histories of individuals who are, in a sense, more real in their daydreams than in their daily lives.

Egon Wolff

Egon Wolff was born in 1926 in Santiago, Chile, to German parents. During his adolescence he was affected by periods of ill health, including tuberculosis and several bouts of pneumonia, but this also had its positive side in the sense that it gave him the opportunity to read widely. Thomas Mann, Kafka, James Joyce and William Faulkner figured prominently amongst the authors he enjoyed at this particular time. The economic circumstances of his family were not, however, sufficiently strong to allow Wolff to devote himself to medicine, which would have required many years of study, and so, as an alternative, he took up Chemical Engineering. Subsequently, he worked in this area, firstly selling cosmetics, then various chemical products, and finally as a partner in a factory which manufactured paint. His writing for the theatre, by far the most extensive of the three authors represented in this collection, was therefore completed in the course of a working life devoted to entirely different matters, though his daily contact with people from different levels of society, workers and bosses alike, clearly allowed him to observe them and draw upon that experience in his plays, as *The Invaders* suggests. Only at the age of 53, however, was Wolff able to focus entirely upon his theatre work, for in 1979 he was appointed to a teaching post in the Escuela de Teatro at the Catholic University in Santiago.

Although Wolff has been less directly involved in politics than Mario Vargas Llosa, much of his work reflects the tensions which have existed in Chile over a long period of time, especially those between the rich and the poor. In the 1950s and 60s — Wolff's first play, *Mansion of Owls*, was performed in 1958 — Chile enjoyed a largely democratic system in which elections were both frequent and highly competitive. Nevertheless, tensions had always existed, as elsewhere in Latin America, between the different classes: in the countryside between the peasants and the landowning elite; in the cities between the workers and the middle classes, a process which manifested itself in particular after

the election of Salvador Allende, communist leader of the
Unidad Popular, in 1970. Winning by a majority of less
than two per cent, Allende's three-year period in office was
opposed at every step by the upper and middle classes and
by the landowners and industrialists, strongly supported by
the right wing American government of the time. On 11
September 1973 the military launched a coup in the course
of which the presidential palace was attacked from the air,
at least 2000 people died, and Allende committed suicide.
The new military government dissolved parliament and
suspended the constitution, thereby inaugurating the
notorious regime of Augusto Pinochet. The first
performance of *Paper Flowers* had taken place in 1970.

While much of Wolff's work derives its power from the
class tensions described above, it is also distinguished by his
exploration of different aspects of human behaviour. In the
early plays, in particular, a dominant mother figure allows
Wolff to focus on family tensions and on the manipulation
of one character by another, both of which are features of
his major plays. Such is the character of Marta in *Mansion of
Owls* (1958), an overprotective mother who lives with her
two sons and whose suffocating relationship with them leads
to disaster; and such is Matilde, who in *Disciples of Fear*
(1958) imposes her will on her husband and her three sons,
insisting on buying a factory which she thinks will bring the
family financial security but which, through a series of
events involving drugs and financial debt, leads to its
disintegration. The theme of the family is developed in
different ways in other plays too. In *Kindergarten* (1977), for
example, Meche visits her brothers, Toño and Mico, after
an absence of ten years. All three reveal signs of repressed or
distorted sexuality, and, thrown together after so many
years, create for each other a living hell. Wolff's fascination
with the psychology of his characters and the pressure they
exert on each other, reminiscent in some respects of the
theatre of Harold Pinter, is to be seen too in plays in which
the family becomes a group of an altogether looser kind.
Such is *Girlmother* (1962), in which eight people, all of whom
have suffered some personal misfortune, live together in a

run-down house, some of them dependent on others, some taking advantage of others, some abused by others. Similarly, in one of Wolff's greatest plays, *The Raft of Medusa* (1984), a group of elegant bourgeois individuals, trapped in an elegant mansion, rather like the characters of Luis Buñuel's great film, *The Exterminating Angel*, are revealed under pressure to resort to behaviour no better than that of the down-and-outs who constantly threaten to invade the house. Here, in effect, is a cross section of Chilean society in which the differences between rich and poor are seen to be largely superficial, a façade which, in the case of the bourgeoisie, Wolff rips away in order to expose the moral corruption beneath.

Paper Flowers, first staged at the Teatro del Callejón in the Sala Mozart de la Municipalidad de Las Condes, Santiago, in 1970, is in some ways a variation on *The Invaders*, first performed in 1963. In this earlier play Lucas Meyer, his wife Pietà, and their two children, Bobby and Marcela, live a life of luxury, but this is gradually taken away from them and Lucas Meyer exposed as a ruthless murderer when their comfortable existence is disrupted by the arrival of a group of starving and homeless down-and-outs.

In *Paper Flowers* Beto, a dishevelled young man of 30 otherwise known as 'El merluza' (in the translation I prefer to call him 'Barracuda' rather than 'Hake', the literal meaning of the word), helps carry the shopping for Eva, a lonely middle-class woman of forty. Invited to take the packages into her kitchen, he asks for a cup of tea and, after some reluctance on her part and a good deal of pleading on his own, persuades her to let him sleep in an armchair. Subsequently, the action unfolds in a manner similar to that of *The Invaders*, for 'Barracuda', like his down-and-out counterparts in the earlier play, gradually takes over Eva's entire life. His callous killing of the canary while she is away from the apartment anticipates the havoc he wreaks both on her and her apartment. By the end of the play she has been reduced to a total automaton, unable to think or act for herself, while around her the once elegant flat has been reduced to rubble. In the final scene, an unnerving parody of the traditional wedding ceremony, 'Barracuda' leads his bride to the riverbank where he and his companions permanently live, and where Eva's happy-ever-after future will now be found.

Regarded by many as Wolff's masterpiece, *Paper Flowers* contains the key themes and situations of his theatre in general: the social divide between rich and poor; the power struggle between individuals; the isolation of the individual; the violence of which human beings are capable; and their need for love and affection. In terms of characterisation, 'Barracuda' is particularly well drawn: cunning, manipulative, ultimately heartless. Eva is his opposite: cultured, refined, straightforward. As for the play in general, the conflict between the two individuals could occur anywhere, and Eva's apartment becomes, as events unfold, a universal battleground.

José Triana

José Triana was born in 1931 in Bayano, Cuba. Between 1934 and 1959, the year of the Cuban Revolution and the beginning of Fidel Castro's domination of Cuban politics, the affairs of the country had been dominated by Fulgencio Batista, a military man and ally of the USA. During this period Batista held power either through puppet presidents or on his own, and in the mid-1950s, as a result of his opposition to the Batista regime, Triana was forced to leave Cuba, choosing to live in Madrid where he engaged in theatre activities of different kinds, sometimes directing, sometimes acting small parts. There he began writing and, in the process, met the Cuban theatre director, Francisco Morín, who encouraged him to consider writing a play on the Medea theme. After Batista's overthrow in 1959, Triana returned to Cuba and, inspired by Morín's example, commenced serious work, producing a first version of the play in 1959-60 and a revised and improved version four years later. It was followed by a number of other plays, including *The Death of Ñeque* (1962, revised 1996), *Night of the*

Assassins (1957-65), *War Ceremonial* (1968-73), *Having Fun on the Battlefield* (1971), and *Worlds Apart* (1979).

In spite of the fact that the Revolution had ended a dictatorship, the Castro regime became, during the course of the 1960s, increasingly authoritarian, demanding that, amongst others, all artists toe the revolutionary line. In 1971, for example, the famous Cuban writer, Heberto Padilla, was obliged to confess to his crimes against the Revolution. As far as Triana was concerned, the Cuban Ministry of Culture saw his work, especially *Night of the Assassins*, as a criticism of the Casto administration and therefore considered him to be 'not one of us'. Consequently, his work was denied the resources necessary for its performance, he became an outsider in the Cuban artistic world, and in 1980 he left Cuba for Paris, where he now lives with his wife.

Triana belongs, as the preceding account suggests, to the generation of Cuban dramatists who in the early 1960s were part of the cultural enthusiasm inspired by the Revolution. In this context, it is hardly surprising that his work should draw heavily on Cuban influences, be they popular theatrical forms, music, language, and the myths, rituals and superstitions associated with Cuban and Afro-Caribbean traditions. On the other hand, having spent some time in Europe, it was inevitable that, like Mario Vargas Llosa and Egon Wolff, he should also be influenced by certain aspects of European theatre, not least by the theatre of the absurd and the so-called 'ceremonial theatre'. As is the case with many dramatists, be they Latin American or European, Triana's work is also often critical of particular aspects of Cuban life, as much of the past as the present. In *The Assassins*, for example, the three young people, Lalo, Cuca and Beba, enact the murder of their parents who, for them, represent the suffocating social and moral values of the Cuban middle classes. In the later *Worlds Apart*, staged by the Royal Shakespeare Company in 1986, Triana sets the action at the turn of the nineteenth century, and in its protagonist Victoria, the daughter of an upper-middle-class landowner, depicts the unhappy fate of a woman born into a patriarchal family in which honour is all important and in which Victoria's adulterous affair cannot be tolerated.

Triana's first version of *Medea in the Mirror*, performed in 1960 at the Sala Teatro Prometeo in Havana, directed by Francisco Morín, was in general a great success, but the third act received a certain amount of criticism and was considerably revised four years later, when the characters of Madam Pitonisa and Doctor Mandinga appeared for the first time. After its first performance it was also presented at other theatres in Havana, as well as on Cuban television. As far as his sources were concerned, Triana familiarised himself with the Medea story in its various dramatic treatments – Euripides, Seneca, Anouilh, and the Spanish writer Miguel de Unamuno, amongst others – but then proceeded to adapt the traditional story to his own ends. In Euripides' play Medea is a princess from Colchis, a sorceress who has married Jason, leader of the Argonauts, after helping him to obtain the Golden Fleece and to bring about the death of his uncle, Pelias, in order to put Jason on the throne. As a result of the murder, however, Jason was obliged to flee and subsequently met and married Creusa, daughter of the King of Corinth. Consumed by her desire for revenge, Medea murders her own children.

Triana's version contains no royal characters. His play is set in a 'solar', the kind of tenement building with which he had been familiar as a boy and which he revisited by way of preparation for writing the play. The characters are a cross-section of the lower end of Cuban society, as well as of Cuba's racial mix. Medea becomes Maria and, far from being a princess, is a 'mulata', the daughter of one white and one black parent. The wife of Antonio is also a 'mulata'. Señorita Amparo is a 'mestiza', the daughter of Indian and white parentage. Erundina, Madam Pitonisa and Doctor Mandinga are black. The barber, Julián, and Perico Piedra Fina are white. As far as the events of the play are concerned, Maria takes the same revenge as Medea and is similarly emotional. Julián, though not heroic in the Jason mould, is just as selfish in abandoning his wife for someone else. And Perico Piedra Fina, far from being a king, is an unscrupulous landlord and crooked entrepreneur, exploiting the poorer Cubans in order to further his own ends.

The action of the play is set a few years before its composition, clearly during the dictatorial regime of Batista, and it can therefore be seen as a political allegory in which Perico Piedra Fina, controlling those around him, is a form of Batista, and Julián, who is only concerned with making money, becomes the equivalent of the better off Cuban whites. In this sense, Maria's revenge on Julián is the equivalent of the Cuban Revolution of 1959. But in a sense the play may also be seen as a veiled warning to the Castro regime of the dangers of becoming too oppressive. In short, the mirror image of the play's title suggests a multiplicity of meanings: not simply that the traditional story of Medea is used as a mirror for a modern version, but that Triana creates in this new play a mirror in which the contemporary social and political situation is reflected. On the other hand, *Medea in the Mirror* is much more than a political allegory, for a much broader resonance is evoked by the introduction into the action of Afro-Caribbean ritual and superstition, as well as music and dance. In consequence, we are left with the feeling that the play's characters are both aware of and subjected to forces outside and more powerful than themselves. In this respect it may be linked to Greek tragedy, in which human beings are often the playthings of the gods, or to more modern European drama – Lorca is a clear example – in which the destinies of men and women are ruled by instinctive forces, as well as by fate.

Triana's play is distinguished, amongst other things, by its characterisation. Maria comes across as a woman torn throughout by conflicting emotions: love for Julián, anxiety over his disappearance, disbelief at the news he has abandoned her, an insatiable desire for revenge, and final desperation. Erundina, her servant, emerges as a practical, common sense woman, the very opposite of Señorita Amparo, whose excessive politeness and refinement lead to a long-windedness which is the source of much comedy. Perico Piedra Fina is a complete cynic, someone who believes that every man has his price and that he, a self-made man, has the fate of others in his hands. And Julián, given a smaller role than Perico, is entirely superficial, an opportunist, a ladies' man whose showy chain and flashy rings embody his nature. In short, the characters of the play are extremely varied and vividly drawn.

In this respect the language of the play is highly effective. Exchanges between characters are sharp and pungent. Soliloquies, as in Maria's case, are full of questions and exclamations, revealing at once her agitated state of mind. In every case rhythm is of crucial importance, in the light of which Triana's comment – 'I have always thought of theatre as a music box, as a poem' – is very revealing. In addition, his language is extremely colourful in terms of its expressions and turns of phrase, vividly rooted in the linguistic traditions of his native Cuba. But, as Triana has observed, he constantly attempts to raise it to a higher level: '. . . I believe that I try to dignify popular speech. I try to raise it to a tragic dimension, that is my aim . . .' His success in this respect is evident throughout *Medea in the Mirror*, both in relation to the characters and to the Chorus, composed of a newspaper-boy, a barber, Antonio's wife, and a bongoman, whose interventions inform and simultaneously energise the onstage events.

The three Latin American plays presented in this collection are, as the preceding comments suggest, characteristic of their authors in terms of their issues, preoccupations, and dramatic style, and, inasmuch as these authors are rooted in the culture and traditions of their individual countries, revealing of that heritage. But, more importantly, these are writers whose intelligence and artistic skills allow them to transcend local frontiers and to offer us visions of Peru, Chile and Cuba in which events and characters take on a much more universal significance, and the plays themselves are seen to be worthy of a place in world drama.

Gwynne Edwards
January 2004

La Chunga

by

Mario Vargas Llosa

Truth is rarely pure and never simple.

Oscar Wilde

To Patricia Pinilla

La Chunga: The play

The story of this play can be summed up in a few words.
Near the Stadium on the outskirts of Piura, a city
surrounded by sand in the north of Peru, La Chunga runs a
tiny bar whose customers are poor and dubious characters.
One night she sees Josefino, one of the regular customers,
arrive with his latest conquest: Meche, an attractive young
woman with a shapely body. La Chunga is immediately
captivated. Josefino, to amuse himself with his friends – a
group of idle individuals who call themselves 'the
Champions' – encourages Meche to provoke La Chunga. In
the course of the night, Josefino loses all his money at dice.
In order to carry on playing, he loans Meche to La Chunga
and both of them spend the rest of the night together in La
Chunga's room, above the bar. What happens between
them? After that night Meche disappears and nothing more
is known of her.

The play begins a long time after Meche's disappearance.
The Champions are playing at dice at the same table, and
they try to worm from La Chunga the truth of what
precisely happened. And since they fail, they invent it. The
images fashioned by each one of them materialise on stage
and contain, perhaps, a fleeting element of the truth. But,
more than anything, they are the hidden truths that dwell
within them. In La Chunga's bar truth and untruth, past
and present, coexist, as they do in the human mind.

The themes developed or touched on in the play, by
means of this story, should be clearly understood: love,
desire, taboos, the relationship between men and women,
the habits and customs of a certain way of life, the role of
women in a primitive and 'macho' society, and the way in
which these objective things are reflected in the world of
imagination. I believe it is clear in the play that external
reality does not subject or subdue desire; on the contrary, it
is thanks to his imagination and desires that even the
humblest of men can for a moment break the prison bars
behind which he is normally confined.

As in my earlier plays – *The Girl From Tacna* and *Kathie and the Hippopotamus* – I have tried to project by means of a dramatic fiction the totality of human actions and dreams, facts and fantasies. The characters of the play are simultaneously themselves and their fantasies, people of flesh and blood whose destinies are conditioned by particular limitations – they are poor, uneducated, on the fringes of society – but who are also spirits for whom, despite the harshness and monotony of their lives, there is always the possibility of relative freedom, which is the province of the imagination, that human attribute *par excellence*.

I use the phrase 'the totality of human actions' to underline the obvious fact that a man is an indivisible unity of acts and desires, and also because this unity must be revealed in the performance, confronting the audience with an integrated world in which the man who speaks and the man who dreams – the man who is, the man who pretends he is – are a single, unbroken whole, two sides of a coin, like reversible garments that never allow us to know which is really the outside or which the inside.

I fail to see why the theatre should not be a suitable medium for the representation of human objectivity and subjectivity fused, or rather, fusing. But there are powerful prejudices which hold that that ambiguous, fleeting, arbitrary, timeless, suddenly changing world that is constructed by imagination and stimulated by desire, cannot exist on a stage together with objective reality without creating insuperable difficulties of staging. I cannot think that this scepticism has any explanation other than the laziness and fear of risk that stifle creative activity.

The aim is simply to create a form of theatre in which theatricality plays an important part, which reveals the human aptitude for pretence, for projecting oneself into situations and characters entirely different from one's own. In the scenes in which the characters live their dreams, they have to indulge themselves, split themselves in two, as actors do upon a stage, as men and women do inside their heads when they call upon imagination to enrich their lives, acting in their imaginations what real life denies them.

To find a dramatic technique – a way of embodying – for something shared by everyone, the way in which we enrich our lives by creating images and fictions should be a stimulating challenge, an act of defiance for those who wish to see the theatre renew itself and explore new avenues, instead of slavishly following the three canonical models of modern theatre, now so overworked that they show every sign of hardening of the arteries: the epic-didactic theatre of Brecht; the amusing games of the theatre of the Absurd; the antics of the 'happening' and other kinds of spectacle without a text. I believe that the theatre and its images constitute a genre privileged to portray the disturbing labyrinth of angels, devils and miracles which is the true abode of our desires.

Mario Vargas Llosa
9 July 1985

La Chunga: characters

Piura, 1945.

La Chunga's bar-restaurant is situated near the Stadium, in
that place where not long ago there sprang up a shanty
town of matting and planks, built on the sandy ground
between the highway to Sullana and the Grau Barracks.
Unlike the flimsy houses around it, La Chunga's house is a
proper building, large and square, its walls of adobe, its roof
of galvanised iron. On the ground floor there are rough
tables, benches and seats for the customers, and a counter
made of planks. Behind this is a grimy and smoky kitchen.
On the first floor, which is reached by a staircase with just a
few stairs, is the room which none of the locals has ever
seen: La Chunga's bedroom. From there La Chunga can
observe all that happens below through a window covered
by a small flower-patterned curtain.

Her customers are people from the locality: soldiers from
the Grau Barracks on their day off, football and boxing fans
who stop on their way to the Stadium to oil their vocal
cords, or workers from the construction firm engaged on the
new development for the whites – Buenos Aires – which is
making Piura even bigger.

La Chunga has a female cook who sleeps by the kitchen
range and a young boy who acts as a waiter during the day.
She is always at the bar counter, usually standing. When, as
is the case tonight, there are few customers – just those four
good-for-nothings who call themselves the Champions and
spend their time rolling dice and drinking beer – La Chunga
is to be seen sitting in her wicker rocking-chair which rocks
gently and squeaks while she stares into space – is she lost in
her memories or is her mind completely blank?

She is a tall, ageless woman. She has a hard expression,
smooth, tight skin, strong bones, vigorous gestures,
unblinking eyes. Her long dark hair is tied with a ribbon, her
mouth is cold, her lips thin, her words are few and she rarely
smiles. She wears blouses with short sleeves and skirts so
lacking in glamour, so ordinary, that they resemble the

uniform of a convent school. Sometimes she goes barefoot, sometimes she wears flat sandals. She is efficient. She runs the place with an iron fist and commands respect. Her appearance, her harshness, her terseness induce fear. Very rarely do the drunks make any advances. She rejects intimacy and flattery and has not been known to have lovers or close friendships. She seems resolved to live alone, wholly dedicated to her business. Leaving aside the brief episode with Meche – confusing enough for the customers, anyway – no one or nothing is known to have changed her routine. As far as the Piuranos who frequent the bar can remember, she is always serious and motionless behind the counter. Does she sometimes go to the Varieties or the Municipal to see a film? Does she go to the Plaza de Armas some evening to a concert? Or to the Eguiguren Pier or the Puente Viejo to bathe in the river – if it has rained in the Cordillera – as summer arrives? Does she watch the military procession on Independence Day with the crowd that gathers at the foot of the Grau Monument?

She is not a woman with whom one can have a conversation; she either answers with monosyllables or a movement of the head. And if the question asked of her is a bit of a joke, her reply can be coarse or extremely crude. As they say in Piura: 'La Chunga doesn't suffer fools.'

The Champions – rolling the dice, toasting, joking at the table directly beneath the oil-lamp suspended from a beam and in whose light the insects fly around – know all this only too well. They are old customers, from the time the bar belonged to a certain Doroteo, with whom La Chunga was at first involved and whom she later threw out (hitting him with a bottle as local gossip has it). But in spite of coming here two or three times a week, the Champions cannot be said to be friends of La Chunga. They are simply acquaintances and customers. Who in Piura could claim to have enjoyed her close friendship? The runaway Meche perhaps? La Chunga has no friends. She is unsociable and solitary, like one of those cacti in the Piuran sand.

Mario Vargas Llosa

This translation of *La Chunga* was first performed at the Old Red Lion, London, on 1 November 1988, with the following cast:

La Chunga	Kristin Millward
Meche	Irina Brook
José	Robert Morgan
Lituma	Jack Elliot
El Mono	Martin Turner
Josefino	James Vaughan

Directed by Keith Hack
Designed by Voytek and Tom Piper
Lighting by Gerry Jenkinson

Act One

Scene One: A Game of Dice

El Mono (*before throwing the dice, he raises his hand*)   Let's sing our song, Champions, so it'll bring me luck.

José, **Lituma**, **Josefino** and **El Mono** *sing in unison, waving their arms.*
> We are unbeatable,
> We don't want to work.
> We'd rather drink,
> We'd rather shirk.
> We are unbeatable,
> We prefer dice,
> And now we are ready
> To play for our lives.

El Mono *blows on the dice, kisses the hand that holds them and rolls them across the table. The black-and-white cubes run, leap, collide with the half-full glasses and come to rest against a bottle of 'Cristal' beer.*

El Mono   Hey, hey, hey! Double three! Fantastic! Double or quits, lads. Which one of you?

No one replies or adds to the notes and coins that **El Mono** *has next to his glass.*

Looks like you're nothing but bloody queers!

He gathers the dice in again, blows on them, shakes them above his head, doesn't throw yet.

Here's another six coming up! Five and a one, four and a two, double three . . . or this champion's about to lose his cock-a-doodle-doo.

Josefino (*gives him a knife*)   Here. You can cut it off with this.

José   Come on, Mono. Roll the dice. It's the only thing you'll ever get to roll.

El Mono (*grimacing*)　Right. Here we go then. Three and a six. (*He crosses himself.*) Give me the six, you fucking saint!

Lituma (*turning away to the bar*)　Mono's a crude bugger, Chunga! Don't you think so?

La Chunga *shows no reaction. She doesn't even bother to look in the direction of the Champions' table.*

José　Why don't you answer poor Lituma, Chunguita? He's asking you a question.

El Mono　Maybe she's dead. Maybe it's only her corpse that's rocking. Are you dead, Chunguita?

La Chunga　That's what you'd like me to be. So you can leave without paying for the drinks.

El Mono　Ha, ha, ha, my nice little Chunga. I've brought you to life again.

He blows on the dice, kisses and rolls them.

Give me the six, you fucking saint.

The four faces follow the troubled journey of the black-and-white cubes between glasses, bottles, cigarettes and matchboxes. This time they roll on to the damp earth floor.

One and a three are four, Champions. I need two more. The kitty's there for the taking if one of you's got balls enough to take me on.

Lituma　What happened that time with Meche, Chunga? There's only us here. Come on, tell us.

José　Tell us, tell us, my nice little Chunga.

La Chunga (*indifferent, her voice sleepy*)　Go and ask your fucking mother. She'll tell you.

El Mono (*rolls the dice*)　The six! The six! Hey, lads, that's put a stop to you! You can choke on that! (*He turns towards the counter.*) Be nasty to me, Chunga. It brings me luck.

He takes the pile of notes and money and kisses them extravagantly.

Another couple of ice-cold bottles. This champion's paying.
Ha, ha, ha.

La Chunga *gets up. The chair continues to rock, its squeaking
regular, while* **La Chunga** *goes to fetch a couple of bottles of beer
from a bucket full of ice which she keeps under the counter. She takes
them across to the table, her manner indifferent, and places them in
front of* **El Mono**. *A forest of bottles litters the table.* **La Chunga**
goes back to the rocking-chair.

José (*his voice piping maliciously*)   Aren't you ever going to tell
us what you did that night with Meche, Chunga?

Josefino   That's enough about Mechita. Or one of you
can take his pants down and do me a big favour. Mention
her name and it gives me a real hard on.

El Mono (*winking, in an effeminate voice*)   Does it do that for
you, Chunguita?

La Chunga   That's enough, you son-of-a-bitch! I'm here
to serve the drinks, not to be the butt of anyone's jokes or
listen to your filth. You just watch it, Mono.

El Mono *begins to shake, his teeth chatter and his shoulders and
arms move. The whites of his eyes show as he is overcome by
uncontrollable contortions.*

El Mono   Oh, I'm scared. I'm scared stiff of her!

The Champions kill themselves laughing. They slap **El Mono**, *to
bring him to.*

Lituma   Keep calm, Chunga. We get you worked up, but
you know we love you.

Josefino   Who the fuck mentioned Meche? Was it you,
Lituma? You've made me think of her again, you prick! (*He
solemnly raises his glass.*) A toast to the tastiest bit of stuff who
ever walked the land of Admiral Grau. To you, Mechita, in
heaven, in Lima, in hell, wherever you are!

Scene Two: Meche

While **Josefino** *is making the toast and the Champions are drinking,* **Meche** *enters, with the slow movement and rhythm of someone who belongs to the world of memory. She is young, with a firm and shapely figure. She wears a thin, tight-fitting dress and high-heeled shoes. As she walks, she flaunts herself.* **La Chunga** *watches her approach and her eyes become much more alive. But the Champions are not aware of her presence.* **La Chunga**, *in contrast, is totally absorbed by this image. It is as if, for her, the present moment has dissolved. The voices of the men become fainter.*

El Mono   I'll never forget your face the first time Meche came here, my lovely little Chunga. You were turned to stone.

Lituma   You're the only one in the world who knows where she is, Chunga. Come on, tell us! It doesn't matter. Put an end to our curiosity.

José   Tell us what happened that night between you and her, Chunguita. Fuck me, it's costing me my sleep.

El Mono   I'll tell you what happened. (*He sings and pulls his usual funny faces.*)
Chunga with Meche
Meche with Chunga
Cheche with Menga
Menga with Cheche
Chu Chu Chu!
And long live Fumanchu!

La Chunga (*her voice lacks energy and seems far away, her eyes fixed in fascination on* **Meche**, *who is now close to her*)   Hurry up and empty your glasses. It's closing-time.

Josefino *gets up unnoticed and, with a leap from the present into the past, from reality to dream, goes over to* **Meche** *and takes her by the arm, like someone who owns her.*

Josefino   Evening, Chunguita. This is Meche.

Meche (*holding out her hand to* **La Chunga**)   Pleased to meet you, señora.

The men acknowledge **Josefino** *and* **Meche** *with a wave, but are wholly absorbed in the game of dice.* **La Chunga**'s *eyes devour* **Meche**. *She continues to hold her hand. Her voice is full of the emotion that the impact of* **Meche** *has made on her.*

La Chunga   So you are the famous Meche? Welcome. I thought this one would never bring you here. I really wanted to meet you.

Meche   Me too, señora. Josefino talks about you a lot. (*Pointing to the table.*) Them too – all the time. About you and this place. I was dying to come. (*Pointing to* **Josefino**.) But he wouldn't bring me.

La Chunga *reluctantly releases* **Meche**'s *hand. She makes an effort to control her feelings and seem natural.*

La Chunga   I can't think why. I haven't eaten anyone yet. (*To* **Josefino**.) Why wouldn't you bring her?

Josefino (*laughing lasciviously*)   I was scared you might take her from me, Chunguita. (*He holds* **Meche** *by the waist and shows her off, proud of himself.*) She's worth her weight in gold, don't you think?

La Chunga (*admiring her, agreeing*)   Yes. I congratulate you this time, you hen-house Don Juan. She's worth all your other women put together.

Meche (*rather abruptly*)   Thank you, señora.

La Chunga   Just call me Chunga. No need to be so formal with me.

Lituma (*calling from the table*)   Are you coming, Josefino? We are going to start another game.

José   Mono's got the dice, Josefino. Make the most of it. He's so stupid, it's easy money for us.

El Mono   Me stupid? I'll take the whole world on tonight with the whore saint on my side. You'll lose so much, Josefino, you'll have to give me Meche as security.

Josefino (*to* **La Chunga**)   How much do you think I'd get for this little piece, Chunguita?

La Chunga   Whatever you ask. You're right, she's worth her weight in gold. (*To* **Meche**.) What would you like? It's on me. Beer? Vermouth?

Josefino   I don't believe it . . . Do you hear that, lads? La Chunga's buying.

La Chunga   Not for you I'm not! You're a regular. I'm buying Meche a drink because she's new. And I want her to come back.

At the table the men are making a great noise.

El Mono (*shouting*)   I never thought I'd see the day.

José (*shouting*)   Ask for a whisky, Meche. Invite the rest of us.

Josefino *goes to the table and sits down with the others.*

Josefino   Right, let's get my hand in.

Meche   Weren't you going to take me to the pictures?

Josefino   Later. I'm going to win my supper first by fleecing these three pricks. The night is young, my sweet.

Meche (*to* **La Chunga**, *pointing to* **Josefino**)   I can see we won't get to the pictures. There's a film at the Varieties with Esther Williams and Ricardo Montalbán . . . in colour . . . with music and bulls . . . If only Josefino wasn't so fond of gambling.

La Chunga (*giving her a vermouth*)   He's got all the vices, that one. The biggest scoundrel any mother ever gave birth to. What do you see in him? What does any woman see in such a layabout? Tell me, Meche. What's his secret?

Meche (*somewhat between blushing and pretending to blush*)
Well, it's difficult to say. He says nice things. And he's not
bad looking, is he? And . . . well . . . when he kisses and
touches me, he makes me tremble. I see little stars.

La Chunga (*with a mocking smile*)   He really makes you see
little stars?

Meche (*laughing*)   Well, in a manner of speaking. You
know what I mean.

La Chunga   I don't know what you mean. How can a
pretty girl like you fall for such a worthless devil? (*Serious.*)
You know what to expect from him, don't you?

Meche   I never think about the future, Chunga. You have
to take love as it comes. Happiness right now, this minute.
Suck the juice while it lasts. (*Suddenly alarmed.*) What can I
expect from him?

La Chunga   He'll make you see little stars for a while
more. But then it'll be the whorehouse, so you can keep him
by selling yourself.

Meche (*taken completely aback*)   What? You must be joking!
Do you think I could do that? You don't know me. Do you
think I'm capable . . . ?

La Chunga   Of course you are! Like all the other silly
girls who saw stars with that pimp.

She reaches out and strokes **Meche***'s cheek.*

Don't look so scared. I like you better when you smile.

Scene Three: The cock-of-the-walk and the three pricks

At the table of the Champions, the game is beginning to get exciting.

El Mono (*very excited*)   A three and a four makes seven! Ha,
ha, ha! Do you still think I'm stupid, José? Get down on

your knees and pray to me, you miserable pricks. Have you seen anything like it in all your miserable lives? Seven hands on the trot. Well, there's the winnings, for anyone who's brave enough. Which one of you then?

Josefino (*producing some notes*)   Right. Do you think I'm scared? Let's see how much. Two hundred, three hundred. Here's three hundred. Roll the dice, deadbeat.

José   You're bloody loaded, Josefino. (*Dropping his voice.*) You must be sending Mechita out to work!

Josefino   Shut up! If she hears you, she'll think something's up. What are you waiting for, Mono?

El Mono *passes the dice in front of his eyes, across his lips, shakes them, charms them.*

El Mono   You're about to suffer, pal. Here we go.

They watch the dice roll, totally absorbed.

Eleven! Come on, lads. The jackpot for me. Fuck it. Eight on the bloody trot! More beer, Chunga, to anoint this miracle.

Josefino (*stopping* **Mono** *as he tries to collect his winnings*)   The kitty stays on the table.

The three men look at him in surprise.

El Mono   If you want to go on losing, it's fine by me, mate. There it is then, if you want to be rich. Six hundred. All on your own, are you?

Josefino   All on my own.

He produces more notes from his pocket, counts them ostentatiously and puts them into the kitty with a dramatic gesture.

There! Six hundred. The-cock-of-the-walk against the pricks.

Lituma   Fuck, he must have robbed a bank or something.

Josefino   Roosters never steal. Not like you pricks. We cocks, we might be bastards, but we aren't thieves.

José   You know very well, Josefino. The cock-run's the worst part of Piura.

Lituma   Don't tell anyone you're a cock, man . . . All you've got is the slaughterhouse, corpses, flies and vultures.

Josefino   But we've got asphalt roads and private streets. You haven't got that here. There's nothing but donkeys and beggars. And everyone shits on the floor next to the bed. I don't know why I mix with you lot. One of these days your shit-smell's going to stick to me. Hang on, Mono. Don't roll the dice yet. Mechita! Come and bring me luck!

Meche *goes over to the table as* **La Chunga** *brings two more beers.* **Josefino** *puts his arm around* **Meche**'s *waist and draws her face down to him. He kisses her on the mouth, displaying his pleasure. The other men laugh and joke.* **La Chunga** *watches them, her eyes bright.*

Josefino   Now then, Mono. Roll the dice.

José (*to* **Josefino**)   Don't you know the saying? 'Lucky in love, unlucky at dice.'

El Mono (*rolling the dice*)   Here we go . . . and I'm going to be rich!

Josefino (*delighted*)   One and a one! You're a dead man, Mono! (*To* **José**.) Wrong, friend! The saying goes: 'Lucky in love, lucky at dice!' A toast to Mechita for the luck she's brought me. Thank you, sweetie! (*He brings her head down again and kisses her, glancing at* **La Chunga** *mockingly*.) Good health, Chunga!

La Chunga *doesn't respond, goes back to the bar.* **El Mono** *holds out his hand to* **Josefino**.

El Mono   Congratulations. You had to have guts to bet against the kitty after eight winning hands. Maybe you are from the cock-run, but you deserve to be one of us.

José (*maliciously*)   Did you see La Chunga's face when Josefino was kissing you, Mechita? Her eyes were popping out of her head.

Lituma   She was green with envy.

Josefino   Can you hear what these deadbeats are saying about you, Chunga?

La Chunga   What?

Josefino   That when I was kissing Meche, your eyes were popping out of your head. You were green with envy.

La Chunga   They're probably right. Who wouldn't envy a woman like her?

Laughter and shouting from the Champions.

Josefino   But you haven't seen her without her clothes, Chunga. Her body's even better than her face. Isn't that right, Meche?

Meche   Shut up, Josefino.

La Chunga   I'm sure that, for once in your life, you aren't telling lies.

Josefino   Of course I'm not telling lies. Lift your skirt up, sweetie! Show her your legs, so she has some idea.

Meche (*feigning more embarrassment than she feels*)   Josefino, the things you come out with!

Josefino *raises his voice a little, giving it a firmness that avoids being harsh but which barely conceals his authority. He makes a show of his power in front of his friends.*

Josefino   Listen to me. If you and me are going to get on together, you have to do what I say. Show your legs to Chunguita.

Meche (*pretending to be upset but, at bottom, attracted to the game*) You do have some funny ideas, Josefino. And you are very bossy too!

She raises her skirt and shows her legs. The Champions applaud.

Josefino (*laughing*)   What do you think, Chunga?

La Chunga   Not bad.

Josefino (*exuding arrogance*)   I can show my girl off naked to these Champions and to Chunga, but they're all like my own brothers so nothing will happen.

He starts to take the money from the kitty he's just won.

El Mono   Just a moment, brother! Only a coward takes his winnings when someone's got the guts to take him on.

Josefino   You want me to play for the kitty? There's twelve hundred there, Mono. How much have you got?

El Mono *searches in his pockets, takes out all the money he has, counts it.*

El Mono   Five hundred. I owe you seven.

Josefino   No one gives IOUs in this game. It's unlucky. (*He takes* **El Mono**'s *hand, where he has a watch.*) Wait. That's why you've got a watch. I'll take it for the seven hundred.

Lituma   Your watch is worth more than that.

El Mono *removes his watch and together with the five hundred places it in the kitty.*

El Mono   But I'm going to win, man. OK, Josefino, roll these dice, and for God's sake lose.

Josefino (*pushing* **Meche** *towards the bar*)   Go and keep La Chunga company while I win the cash and the watch. I don't need you to bring me luck when I've got the dice. I can make my own.

José   Take care La Chunga doesn't try to have you, Mechita. You've driven her crazy.

Meche (*lowering her voice, she betrays an unhealthy curiosity*)   Is she one of those?

Lituma   No one thought she was until now. We thought she was sexless.

José   But since she saw you she's lost her cool. She's given herself away: she's bloody butch.

Meche   You think so?

Josefino   Aren't your ears burning, Chunga? If you knew what they were saying, you'd take a bottle to them and they'd never set foot in your place again.

La Chunga   What are they saying?

Josefino   José says you've gone crazy seeing Mechita, that you're obviously butch, and Meche wants to know if you really are.

Meche   It's not true, Chunga. Don't believe him. You're a sod, Josefino!

La Chunga   She can come and ask me. I'll tell her when we're alone.

Laughter and wisecracks from the Champions.

Josefino   Go on, sweetie! Flirt with her a bit. Let her get ideas.

El Mono   Are you going to roll those dice, Josefino?

Meche *goes to the bar where* **Chunga** *is standing.*

Scene Four: Butch and feminine

Meche (*bewildered*)   You didn't believe him, did you? You know Josefino's always playing the fool. I didn't say that.

La Chunga   Don't worry. I couldn't care less what people say. (*She shrugs her shoulders.*) If they enjoy it, let them say what they want. So long as I don't hear it . . .

Meche   Doesn't it matter that they say bad things about you?

La Chunga   All that matters to me is that they don't fight, and that they pay for what they drink. As long as they keep quiet and don't smash the place up, they can say what they want.

Meche   Don't you mind them saying you are . . . that?

La Chunga   What? Butch? (*She takes* **Meche** *by the arm.*) What if I am? Would you be afraid?

Meche (*laughing nervously, half meaning, half pretending to mean what she says*)   I don't know. I've never met a real one. They say there are lots of them around, but I've never seen one. (*She looks at* **La Chunga**.) I always thought they were like men. Ugly. You aren't like that at all.

La Chunga   What am I like?

Meche   You're a bit hard, maybe. I suppose you have to be to run a place like this, with all kinds of people and drunks. But you aren't ugly. If you did yourself up a bit, you'd look smart, even handsome. Men would go for you.

La Chunga (*with a dry little laugh*)   I'm not interested in pleasing men. (*She moves her face close to* **Meche**.) But you, oh yes, I'd like to please you. It's the only thing that matters to you, isn't it? Tarting yourself up, painting yourself, making yourself pretty. Turning their heads, getting them worked up.

Meche   That's what being a woman means.

La Chunga   That's what being a fool means.

Meche   In that case all the women in the world are fools.

La Chunga   Most of them are. That's why they end up like they do. They let themselves be pushed around, nothing but slaves to their men. And what for? So that when they get tired of them, they can throw them on the rubbish-heap like dirty rags. (*Pause. She strokes her face again.*) I dread to think what your life will be like when Josefino's tired of you.

Meche   He'll never get tired of me. I'll learn how to keep him happy.

La Chunga   I've seen how you do it: letting him wrap you around his little finger. Aren't you ashamed to be bossed about like that?

Meche   I enjoy doing what he wants. That's what love is.

La Chunga   You mean you'd do anything the wretch asked you to?

Meche   While I still loved him. Anything.

Pause. **La Chunga** *looks at her, silently, and we detect a certain admiration, in spite of herself. Both of them are drawn to the noise created by the Champions.*

Scene Five: Security

El Mono (*euphoric, his fists full of notes*)   Shoo, shoo, shoo. I'm making history. Pinch me, so I know I'm not dreaming, lads.

José (*slapping* **Josefino**)   The game's not finished, Mono. Leave the kitty on the table.

El Mono   What are you going to bet with? You've lost two thousand, your watch, your fountain pen. What the fuck else have you got?

Pause. **Josefino** *looks around the room. He sees* **La Chunga** *and* **Meche**. *His mind made up, he gets to his feet. He walks determinedly across to* **La Chunga**, *his expression that of a man prepared to do anything to satisfy a whim.*

Josefino   Chunguita, I need three thousand to put against the kitty.

La Chunga   You know I'd rather be dead than lend you a cent.

Josefino   I've got security worth more than three thousand. (*He holds* **Meche** *by the waist.*)

Meche *takes it as a joke, though she doesn't quite know how to react.*

Meche   What do you mean?

La Chunga *starts to laugh.* **Josefino** *is very serious. The Champions are silent, watching, fascinated.* **Josefino** *holds* **Meche** *tight against him as if he owns her.*

Josefino   You heard me. You love me, don't you? I love you too. That's why I'm asking you. Didn't you promise you'd always do what I say? Well, you can prove it to me now.

Meche (*open-mouthed, incredulous*)   Have you gone mad? Do you know what you are saying? Or has the beer gone to your head?

Josefino (*to* **La Chunga**)   There's no point in pretending, Chunga. As soon as you saw Meche, I knew you'd gone soft on her. What do you say?

El Mono   Hell! He really means it, lads.

José   Fuck, he's selling her.

Lituma   Why don't you buy her for yourself, Mono? She's worth that three thousand.

Josefino (*without taking his eyes off* **Chunga** *and still holding* **Meche** *tight*)   I wouldn't let Mono have her for all the gold in the world. Nor any other man. (*Kissing* **Meche**.) I'd be too jealous of him. Anyone lays a finger on her, I'll have his guts. (*To* **Chunga**.) I'm not jealous of you, so I'll lend her to you, because I know you'll give her back to me intact.

Meche (*snivelling, confused, exasperated*)   Let me go! I want to get out of here. You good-for-nothing!

Josefino (*releasing her*)   Go on then! But for good! If you go now, you'll have betrayed me, Meche, I'd never forgive you for letting me down when I really needed you.

Meche   But, Josefino. Do you know what you're asking? What do you think I am?

La Chunga (*to* **Meche**, *teasingly*)   And you so sure you'd do whatever this rogue asked you to!

Josefino (*embracing* **Meche**)   Is that what you said? It's settled then. (*He kisses* **Meche**.) I love you, girl. You and me, we'll be together to the end of the world. Don't be silly! No need to cry. (*To* **Chunga**.) What do you say?

La Chunga (*serious; a long pause*)   Let me hear her say she's willing. I want her to say that from now till daybreak she'll do whatever I want.

Josefino (*to* **Meche**)   Don't let me down now. I need you. She won't do anything to you. She's a woman. What can she do, eh?

An emotional pause during which the Champions and **La Chunga** *focus on* **Meche***'s inner struggle. She grips her arms and looks from one to the other.*

Meche (*to* **La Chunga**, *stammering*)   I'll do what you tell me to until daylight.

La Chunga *goes to get the money from beneath the bar.* **Josefino** *whispers to* **Meche** *and caresses her. The Champions begin to recover from the surprise.* **La Chunga** *gives the money to* **Josefino**.

El Mono   Fuck my mother, I really don't believe it. I can't believe my eyes.

Lituma   I'd be willing to marry a woman like that.

José   Fuck it, let's sing our song in honour of Mechita.

El Mono   The song, and a toast to Mechita, lads.

El Mono, **Lituma** *and* **José** *sing.*
    We are unbeatable
    We don't want to work
    We'd rather drink
    We'd rather shirk

We are the Champions
We prefer dice,
But now a toast
To the girl we like:
Mechita!

They raise their glasses to **Meche** *and drink.* **La Chunga** *takes* **Meche***'s hand and leads her to her room, both of them climbing the short flight of stairs.* **Josefino** *counts the money and returns to the table where the game is taking place.*

Act Two

Scene One: The Champions

The positions of the actors are identical to those at the beginning of Act One. We are in the present, a long time after the episode concerning **Meche**. *The Champions are playing dice at their table under the lamp hanging from a beam, and* **La Chunga** *is sitting in her rocking-chair, her eyes staring into space. The sounds of the town come and go in the warm night air: the chirping of crickets, a car in the night, the barking of dogs and the braying of a donkey.*

José   How much do you think I'd have to pay La Chunga to know what happened that night with her and Meche?

Lituma   She wouldn't tell you for a million. She'll never tell you. Forget it, José.

Josefino   She'd tell me if I asked her. For nothing.

El Mono   A real tough guy, eh, Josefino?

Josefino   Do you think I'm joking? (*He takes out his knife and makes it glint in the light of the lamp.*) La Chunga may be more like a man, but there's no man or woman who won't talk like a parrot with this against their throat.

El Mono   Can you hear what he's saying, Chunga?

La Chunga (*with her usual indifference*)   Finish your drinks quickly. It's closing-time.

Josefino   Don't worry, Chunguita. If I wanted to, I'd make you tell me everything about that night. But I don't want to, so you can shove your secret up your arse. I don't want to know. I couldn't care less about Meche. Out of sight, out of mind. The woman's not been born that I'd run after.

José *has stood up and, without the other men noticing, he moves towards* **La Chunga**'s *rocking-chair. He has a fixed expression and his mouth is half-open, like someone sleepwalking. Throughout the* *following scene, the men behave as if* **José** *still occupied the empty seat: they touch glasses with this invisible* **José**, *take his bets, pass him the dice, slap him on the back, joke with him.*

José (*his voice full of emotion*)   Something changed for me that night, Chunga, though nobody knows it. (*He punches his head.*) I can see it clearly, here, as if it were still happening. I remember everything that you and Meche said. When you were taking her there – to your room – my heart was beating fast. (*He makes* **La Chunga** *touch his chest.*) Can you feel it? Can you feel how fast it's beating? As if it's about to burst. It's always the same when I think of the two of you up there.

La Chunga's *lips move as she says something without articulating it.* **José** *strains to hear her but immediately thinks better of it. For a few moments* **La Chunga** *continues to mouth silently the same word. Finally she speaks extraordinarily softly.*

La Chunga   You're a fool, José.

José (*anxious and impatient, pointing to the room*)   Come on, speak. Tell me, Chunguita. What happened? What was it like?

La Chunga (*she lectures him but not severely, as she would a naughty boy*)   You don't really like women of flesh and blood, José. You prefer to remember, to invent them. (*She touches his head, as if she were soothing it.*) The ones in here. Am I right?

José *attempts to make* **La Chunga** *rise from her rocking-chair. He becomes more and more excited.*

José   You took her by the arm, you led her across there. You were climbing the stairs, holding her by the arm. Were you squeezing it? Were you pinching her slowly?

La Chunga *gets up and* **José** *takes her place in the rocking-chair. He tilts it in order to see better.* **La Chunga** *pours vermouth into a glass. She goes up the stairs and into the little room which is bathed in a reddish light.*

Scene Two: The voyeur's dream

Meche (*with a nervous laugh*)   What's going to happen now? What sort of game is this, Chunga?

La Chunga *is now transformed from the cold woman of the earlier scenes into someone who is full of life and sensuality.*

La Chunga   It's not a game. I've paid three thousand for you. You belong to me for the rest of the night.

Meche (*in a challenging tone*)   You mean I'm your slave?

La Chunga   For a few hours at least. (*Offering her the glass.*) To calm your nerves.

Meche (*taking the glass and swallowing most of its contents*)   Do you think I'm nervous? Don't fool yourself. I'm not afraid of you. I'm doing this for Josefino. If I wanted to, I could push you off and run away.

La Chunga *sits on the bed.*

La Chunga   But you won't do that. You said you'd obey me, and I'm sure you're a woman of your word. Anyway, your curiosity's killing you. Right?

Meche (*emptying the glass*)   If you think two vermouths are going to get me drunk, you can forget it. I've a good head for drink. I can drink for a whole night and my head's still clear. I can even take more than Josefino.

Pause.

La Chunga   Do to me what you do to him when you want to excite him.

Meche (*with the same nervous laugh*)   I can't. You're a woman. You are La Chunga.

La Chunga (*suggestively but authoritatively*)   I am Josefino. Do to me what you do to him.

In the distance we hear soft, tropical music – boleros by Leo Marini or Los Panchos. It suggests couples dancing close together in a place full of smoke and alcohol. **Meche** *begins to undress slowly, with a certain awkwardness. She speaks with some difficulty, lacks assurance.*

Meche   Do you like watching me undress? Like this, slowly? It's the way he likes it. Do you think I'm pretty? Do you like my breasts? My legs? Look how firm my body is. No spots, no pimples, no rolls of fat. None of the things that make a girl ugly. (*She is down to her slip. She hesitates. Her face slips into a sulk.*) I can't, Chunga. You aren't him. I don't believe what I'm doing or saying. I feel stupid, all of this seems so false, so . . .

She slumps down on the bed, head down, confused, wanting and not wanting to cry. **La Chunga** *gets up and sits beside her. She acts with sensitivity now, as if* **Meche**'*s discomfort moved her.*

La Chunga   The truth is I admire you for being here. You surprised me, you know. I didn't think you'd agree. (*She smooths* **Meche**'*s hair.*) Do you love Josefino so much?

Meche (*her voice a whisper*)   Yes, I do. (*Pause.*) Only I don't think I did it just for him. Like you said, I was curious. (*Turning to look at* **La Chunga**.) You gave him three thousand! It's a fortune.

La Chunga (*drawing her hand across* **Meche**'*s face, drying non-existent tears*)   You are worth more.

A touch of flirtatiousness begins to appear slowly out of **Meche**'*s sulkiness and shame.*

Meche   You really like me, Chunga?

La Chunga   You know I do. Didn't you realise?

Meche   Yes. You looked at me like no woman's ever looked at me. You made me feel . . . strange.

La Chunga'*s hand moves over* **Meche**'*s shoulder. She draws* **Meche** *close and kisses her.* **Meche** *allows herself to be kissed, as though she were helpless. When they separate,* **Meche** *laughs, a false laugh.*

La Chunga   It couldn't have been that bad if you can laugh at it.

Meche   How long have you been like that? I mean, have you always been a lesbian? Were you always fond of women?

La Chunga   It's not women I like. It's you.

La Chunga *embraces* **Meche** *and kisses her.* **Meche** *remains unresponsive to* **La Chunga**'*s embrace, allowing herself to be kissed.* **La Chunga** *draws back a little but without releasing* **Meche**, *and commands her.*

La Chunga   Open your mouth, slave.

Meche *laughs a forced laugh but parts her lips.* **La Chunga** *kisses her long and slow and this time* **Meche**'*s arm comes up and encircles* **La Chunga**'*s neck.*

La Chunga   That's more like it. I thought you didn't know how. (*Sarcastically.*) Did you see little stars?

Meche (*laughing*)   Don't make fun of me.

La Chunga (*holding her in her arms*)   I'm not making fun. Tonight I want you to enjoy yourself more than you ever did with that pimp.

Meche   He's not a pimp! Don't call him that. He loves me. Perhaps we'll get married.

La Chunga   He is a pimp. He sold you to me tonight. And later on he'll take you down to the brothel so you can start whoring for him, just like all the other girls he's had.

Meche *wants to break out of* **La Chunga**'*s embrace, pretending to be angrier than she actually is, but after a short struggle she stops.* **La Chunga** *moves even closer and speaks to her, almost kissing her.*

La Chunga   Let's not talk about that good-for-nothing. Only about you and me.

Meche (*calmer*)   Don't hold me so tight. You're hurting me.

La Chunga   I can do what I want with you. You are my slave. (**Meche** *laughs*.) Don't laugh. Say after me: 'I am your slave.'

Pause. **Meche** *laughs. She is serious again.*

Meche   It *is* a game, isn't it? All right. I'm your slave.

La Chunga   'I am your slave and now I want to be your whore.' (*Pause.*) Say it.

Meche (*softly*)   I'm your slave and now I want to be your whore.

La Chunga (*making* **Meche** *lie on the bed and starting to undress*)   So you shall.

La Chunga*'s room becomes dark again and disappears. From the rocking-chair* **José** *continues to look at the darkened room as though hypnotised. We begin to hear the noise created by the Champions at the table – toasts, singing, swearing.*

Scene Three: Speculation about Meche

The whole of the following dialogue takes place while the Champions are rolling dice and drinking beer.

Lituma   Do you want to know something? Sometimes I think that Meche's disappearance is one of Josefino's stories.

El Mono   Set it to music. I don't understand you.

Lituma   A woman can't vanish into thin air between dusk and dawn. Anyway, Piura's a pocket handkerchief.

Josefino   If she was still in Piura, I'd have found her. She's gone somewhere else. Ecuador maybe. Or Lima. (*Pointing to the rocking-chair where* **José** *is sitting*.) She knows where, but you'll take the secret to the grave with you, won't you, Chunguita? It's your fault I've lost a woman who would have made me rich. Even so, I don't hold any grudges. A heart of gold, eh?

El Mono   Don't go on about Mechita. It'll finish José off. (*Elbowing the invisible* **José**.) Drives you crazy, eh, brother? Thinking of them up there all lovey-dovey?

Lituma (*pursuing the topic doggedly*)   Someone would have seen her take a bus or a taxi. She would have said goodbye. She'd have taken her things from the house, but she left her clothes, and her suitcase. No one saw her. So it's by no means certain she's gone away. Do you know what I think sometimes, Josefino?

El Mono (*touching* **Lituma**'*s head*)   You mean you have thoughts? I thought that asses only brayed. Hee-haw!

Josefino   What *do* you think, Einstein?

Lituma   Didn't you used to beat her up? Don't you beat up all the girls who go crazy on you? Sometimes I wonder if you lost control, friend.

Josefino (*laughing*)   You mean I killed her? What a profound thought, Lituma.

El Mono   That miserable rooster wouldn't harm a fly, brother. Look at him. He's all talk, with his knife and his airs. King of the pimps. I only have to blow on him and he'll fall down. I'll show you! (*He blows.*) Fall down! Don't show me up in front of my friends.

Lituma (*very serious, developing his thoughts*)   You might have been jealous because Mechita spent the night with La Chunga. You were crazy, remember you'd even lost your shirt. You went back home like an animal. You needed to let off steam. Mechita was there, so she paid the price. Maybe you did lose control.

Josefino (*amused*)   What did I do then? Cut her up into little bits and throw her in the river? Fuck me, you're a genius, Lituma. (*Passing the dice to the absent* **José**.) Right, José, it's your turn to win. The dice are yours.

Lituma   The things we have to put up with from our friends. If you weren't one of the Champions, I'd cut your balls off and throw them to the dogs, brother.

El Mono   What have the little dogs done to you to make you want to poison them, man?

José *goes back to his seat as quietly as he left it. At the same time, and without the others noticing it,* **Lituma** *gets up and moves away from them.*

Josefino (*to* **José**)   Why are you so quiet, friend?

José   Because I'm losing. I don't want to talk. But my luck's going to change now. (*He picks up the dice and blows on them. He puts a note on the table.*) A hundred. Who'll play me? (*He directs his remark to* **Lituma**'s *chair, as if he were still there.*) You, Lituma?

In the two scenes that follow, **José**, **El Mono** *and* **Josefino** *act as if* **Lituma** *is still with them. But he is in reality at the foot of the stairs, observing* **La Chunga**'s *room which is now illuminated.*

Scene Four: Procuring

La Chunga *and* **Meche** *are fully dressed. There is not the slightest indication that they have undressed and made love. Their attitude towards each other is also entirely different from the previous scene.* **Meche** *is sitting on the bed, a little downcast, and* **La Chunga** *stands in front of her. She does not now strike us as a sensual and commanding woman but as rather enigmatic and Machiavellian.* **Meche** *is smoking a cigarette. She takes a long, slow puff, attempting to conceal her unease.*

Meche   If you think he's going to pay back the three thousand, you must be dreaming.

La Chunga   I know he won't pay it back. It doesn't matter.

Meche (*looking at her, intrigued*)   Think I believe that,
Chunga? You are the greediest woman I've ever known, you
work like a packhorse, night and day, so you can earn more
and more.

La Chunga   I mean it doesn't matter in this case.
Anyway, it's better for you. If I hadn't given him the money,
he'd have taken it out on you.

Meche   Yes. He'd have beaten me. Whenever something
doesn't go his way, whenever he's in a temper, I have to pay
for it. (*Pause.*) One of these days he's going to kill me.

La Chunga   So why do you stay with him? Are you
stupid?

Meche   I don't know . . . Maybe because I *am* stupid.

La Chunga   And you still love him in spite of all the
beatings?

Meche   I don't know any more if I do. I did at first. Now
maybe I stay because I'm afraid, Chunga. He's an animal.
Sometimes, even when I haven't done anything to him, he
makes me kneel in front of him, as if he's a god. He takes his
knife out and draws it across here. 'Thank me for being
alive,' he says. 'Always remember, you owe your life to me.'

La Chunga   And you stay with him? What stupid
creatures women can be! I'll never understand how you can
lower yourself so much.

Meche   You can never have been in love.

La Chunga   Nor will I ever be. I'd rather live without a
man, like a hermit. But no one will ever make me kneel, or
tell me I owe him my life.

Meche   If I could only get away from Josefino . . .

La Chunga *begins to weave a web which attracts the fly to the trap
prepared for it.*

La Chunga   Of course you can, silly! (*Smiling at her wickedly.*) Have you forgotten how pretty you are? Don't you know what you do to men when you pass by? Don't they shower you with compliments? Don't they proposition you when he can't hear them?

Meche   Yes. If I'd wanted to, I could have cheated on him a thousand times. I've had plenty of chances.

La Chunga (*sitting beside her*)   Of course. But maybe you didn't spot the best one.

Meche (*startled*)   Who do you mean?

La Chunga   Someone who's mad about you. Someone who'd do whatever you wanted just to be with you, because he thinks you are the most beautiful, gorgeous woman ever. A queen. A goddess. You can have him worship at your feet, Meche. He'll never treat you badly and you'll never feel scared of him.

Meche   But who is it?

La Chunga   Can't you guess? You should, because he's very timid with women . . .

Meche   Now I know why you gave Josefino the three thousand. Not because you're a lesbian. You're a go-between, Chunga.

La Chunga (*laughing, friendly*)   Do you think I'd pay three thousand to make love to you? No, Mechita. There's no man or woman I'd pay that much for . . . In fact, the money isn't mine. It belongs to the man who loves you. To have you he's willing to spend all he's got, as well as what he hasn't. Be nice to him. Remember you promised to do what I ask. Now you've a chance to get your own back on Josefino for the times he's beaten you. Make the most of it.

Lituma *has come up the stairs and is standing at the entrance to the room, not daring to enter.* **La Chunga** *goes to meet him.*

Come in. Here she is. She's yours. Don't worry, I've spoken to her. Come on, don't be afraid. She's all yours. Enjoy yourself.

With a mocking laugh she goes out of the room and sits down again in the rocking-chair. The Champions carry on playing and drinking.

Scene Five: A Romantic love

Meche (*amazed*)   Fancy it being you. The last person I'd have thought of. El Mono or José, maybe. They're always flirting, and when Josefino's not looking, they go further than that. But you, Lituma, you've never said a word to me.

Lituma (*deeply disturbed*)   I never dared, Mechita. I've always hidden my feelings. But, but I . . .

Meche (*amused by his embarrassment and awkwardness*)   You are sweating, your voice is shaking, you are dying of shame. You *are* funny, Lituma.

Lituma (*pleading*)   Don't make fun of me, Mechita, please, for the sake of whatever you care for most.

Meche   Have you always been afraid of women?

Lituma (*despondently*)   I'm not afraid. It's just that . . . I don't know how to talk to them. The others know how to talk to a girl in the street, how to get off with her. I've never been able to. I get nervous. I can't get the words out.

Meche   Haven't you ever had a girlfriend?

Lituma   I've never had a woman for nothing, Mechita. Only the tarts at the whorehouse. Always for money.

Meche   Yes, well, you are paying for me too.

Lituma (*kneeling in front of* **Meche**)   Don't compare yourself with those tarts, Mechita. Not even as a joke.

Meche   What are you doing?

Lituma   I'd never make you kneel at my feet like Josefino. I'd spend my life on my knees for you. To me you're a queen.

He kneels and tries to kiss her feet.

Meche   Stop it, you look like a dog down there.

Lituma (*attempting to kiss her feet*)   I'll even be that for you if you let me. Your dog, Mechita. I'll obey you. I'll show you affection when you want, or be quiet if you prefer. Don't laugh, I'm being serious.

Meche   Would you really do anything for me?

Lituma   Try me.

Meche   Would you kill Josefino if I asked you to?

Lituma   Yes.

Meche   But he's your friend, isn't he?

Lituma   To me you are worth more than friendship. Do you believe me, Mechita?

Meche *places her hand on his head, as if stroking an animal.*

Meche   Come and sit down. I don't like anyone making a fool of themselves for me.

Lituma *sits on the bed beside her, but doesn't dare to move close to her, much less to touch her.*

Lituma   I've loved you since the day I saw you first, in the River Bar in the Viejo Puente. Don't you remember? No, why would you remember? I've always felt you couldn't see me, even if you were looking.

Meche   In the River Bar?

Lituma   José, El Mono and me . . . we had a game going. And then Josefino came in with you on his arm. (*Imitating him.*) 'Look what I've gone and found myself. Do you like my little woman?' He lifted you up by the waist and showed you off to everyone. (*His face darkens.*) When he does things like that to you, I hate him.

Meche   Does he make you jealous?

Lituma   He makes me envious. (*Pause.*) Tell me, Mechita. Is it true he's got one as big as this? Is that why all the girls are after him? He spends all his time boasting to us about it: 'Mine's as big as a mule's, lads.' But I went and asked the girls and they tell me it's a lie. They reckon it's only average, like most people.

Meche   You won't get round me by telling me all that filth, Lituma.

Lituma   Sorry. You're right. I shouldn't have asked you that. But do you think it's fair? Josefino treats women like dirt. He kicks them around, makes them fall for him, and when he's softened them up, he turns them into whores. But even so, he gets the girls he fancies. As for me, I'm a decent person, a romantic, I'd handle the woman who loved me like a piece of glass. But no one takes any notice of me. Is that fair?

Meche   Maybe it's not. But don't you think life is full of unfairness?

Lituma   Is it because I'm ugly that they don't look at me, Mechita?

Meche (*teasing*)   Let's see. Let me look at you. No, you aren't that ugly, Lituma.

Lituma   Stop making fun. I've never said these things to anyone else.

Meche (*looking at him, with curiosity*)   Did you fall for me the first time you saw me?

Lituma (*agreeing*)   I couldn't sleep the whole night long. I kept on seeing you in the dark. 'She's so pretty. You only see women like her at the pictures.' I got so carried away, I started crying, Mechita. You don't know how many nights I've been awake, thinking about you.

Meche   And you tell me you don't know what to say to women. What you are saying to me is really nice.

Lituma *puts his hand in his pocket and produces a small photograph.*

Lituma   Look. I always carry it with me.

Meche   Where did you get it?

Lituma   I stole it from Josefino. It's lost its colour because I've been kissing it so much.

Meche (*stroking his head again*)   Why didn't you say anything, stupid?

Lituma   We've still got time, haven't we? Marry me, Mechita. We can leave Piura. We can start a new life.

Meche   But you're almost starving to death, Lituma. Like all the gang. You've never done a day's work.

Lituma   Because there was no one to make me change my way of life. But don't think I like being one of the gang. Let's get married and you'll see how much I'll change, Mechita. I'll work hard, at anything. You'll never need anything.

Meche   Would we go to Lima?

Lituma   Yes, Lima. Or wherever you say.

Meche   I've always wanted to see Lima. It's such a big city, Josefino would never find us.

Lituma   Of course he wouldn't. Anyway, what does it matter if he does find us? Are you scared of him?

Meche   Yes.

Lituma   With me you won't be. Dogs that bark don't bite. I know him well, since he was a kid. He's not a deadbeat like us. He's a cockerel. And cockerels are good for nothing but show.

Meche   He's more than show with me. Sometimes he hits me until I pass out. He'll kill me if I leave him for you.

Lituma   Don't be stupid, Mechita. He'll find another girl straight away. Let's go to Lima. Tonight.

Meche (*tempted*)   Tonight?

Lituma   On the night train from La Cruz de Chalpón. Come on.

Meche   And we'll get married?

Lituma   I promise, when we get to Lima. The first thing we'll do. Are you coming? Let's go.

Meche (*pause*)   All right. We'll never come back to Piura. I hope I won't be sorry for this one day, Lituma.

Lituma (*kneeling again*)   Never, Mechita. I swear. Thanks. Thanks. Ask me for something. Anything you want. Tell me to do something.

Meche   Get up. We mustn't waste time. Move, get your case ready. Buy the tickets. Wait for me at the booking-office in La Cruz de Chalpón. It's halfway down Grau Avenue, isn't it? I'll be there, before twelve.

Lituma   Where are you going?

Meche   I can't go with nothing. I'm going to get my things. At least the things I need.

Lituma   I'll come with you.

Meche   No, there's no need. Josefino's gone to the whorehouse. He won't be back till daylight. I'll have plenty of time. They mustn't see us together in the street. They mustn't be able to gossip about us.

Lituma (*kissing her hands*)   Mechita, my lovely Mechita. Such happiness can never be certain. (*He crosses himself, looks* *to the heavens.*) Thank you, dear God, I'm going to change my ways. I'll stop being a good-for-nothing, I'll give up gambling. I'll stop causing trouble. I swear that . . .

Meche (*pushing him*) Come on. Hurry. We are wasting time, Lituma. Quickly.

Lituma Yes, right. Whatever you say, Mechita.

He gets up, hurries, runs, dashes down the stairs, but then slows, hesitates, stops. Slowly, wearily, he goes back to the table without the men responding in any way. The dice, the toasts, the oaths are again the focus of attention.

Scene Six: Speculating about a crime

El Mono Why not? Lituma's right. It could have happened like that. Close your eyes and imagine Mechita. She's going into the house quickly, she's looking this way and that. Her little arse is twitching with fear.

José She's starting to put things in her case, tr–tr–trembling, st–st–stumbling, fa–fa–falling over herself for fear the Great Pimp will suddenly turn up. And she's so scared, the little tips of her little titties are hard as little stones. Very tasty!

Josefino (*laughing*) What then? Go on! What happened then?

Lituma You turned up, before she'd finished packing.

Josefino And I killed her because I found her packing?

El Mono That was just an excuse. You did it because you were pissed off with everyone. Remember, I'd just taken the shirt off your back. Just give me another hand like you did that night, you fucking saint!

José Or because you were jealous. Meche suddenly told you La Chunga had made her happy, so she was going to live with her.

Josefino   I wouldn't have killed her for that. I'd have sent
La Chunga flowers, and a card with a message: 'You've
won. All the best.' I'm a fucking gentleman, lads.

La Chunga (*from her rocking-chair, yawning*)   It's almost
twelve. I'm tired. I shan't tell you again.

Lituma   Be quiet, Chunga. You're interrupting my flow
of thought. When you saw her half-packed, you said:
'Where are you going?' And she said: 'I'm leaving you.'

Josefino   Why would she leave me? Was she fed up to the
back teeth?

Lituma (*serious, thoughtful, without hearing him*)   'I'm leaving
you because I've fallen for a better man than you.'

Josefino   Better than me? So where do you find such a
treasure, eh?

Lituma   'Someone who won't beat me up, who'll be
straight with me, who'll be good to me, who isn't a fucking
cunt and a pimp. Someone good and honest, and on top of
that he'll marry me.'

Josefino   What a stinking rotten imagination, lads! You
can't even think of a good reason why I should kill Mechita.

Lituma   It was as if she was Judas, Josefino. You went at
her, like a mad thing. Maybe you only wanted to rough her
up. But you lost control and there she was, poor kid.

Josefino   So what the fuck did I do with the body?

El Mono   Threw it in the river.

Josefino   It was September. The Piura was dry. So what
did I do with the body? Come on, guess what my perfect
crime was.

José   You buried it in the sand behind your house.

El Mono   You threw it to those German dogs that guard
Señor Beckman's warehouse. They wouldn't even leave the
bones.

José   Right, I'm tired of playing party games. Let's wet our whistles in the brothel, eh?

Josefino   Do you need to go so far when you've got La Chunga here? Come on, give her what she wants.

La Chunga   There's someone else can give the mother-fucker what he wants, Josefino. Much better than me!

Josefino   You leave my mother's name out of it, Chunga. That's one thing I won't stand for.

La Chunga   Leave my name out of it, then.

El Mono   Take no notice of him, Chunguita. You know he's not one of us. He's a rooster.

José   Don't get so worked up, Chunga. Not with us. We love you, you're our lucky mascot.

El Mono *gets up. Without his friends noticing he goes across to* **La Chunga**.

El Mono   These comedians are always stirring it up, Chunga. You'll have to excuse them, they don't know what they are doing. Not me, though. I behave myself. I expect you've noticed. I don't make you see red. I don't make fun of you. I don't go along with them when they mess you about. I'm very fond of you, Chunga.

La Chunga (*looking at him pityingly*)   No need to put on this goody-goody act for me. What's the point if I'm going to let you enjoy yourself. Come on, give me your hand.

She takes him by the hand and leads him to the stairs. She goes up with him. **El Mono** *is happy, his eyes sparkling like a child about to realise a great ambition. The men go on playing with* **Mono**'s *ghost.*

Scene Seven: A naughty boy

Meche   Hello, Monito.

El Mono   Hello, Mechita.

La Chunga   Come in. Don't be scared. We aren't going to beat you up.

El Mono   I know you are both nice people.

Meche   Come here. Sit next to me.

El Mono *sits on the bed next to* **Meche**, *and* **La Chunga** *sits next to him. The two women behave towards* **El Mono** *as if he were a spoilt child, while his facial expressions and gestures suggest his return to infancy. He sighs, then sighs again, as if something bothers him, something he wants to share with them but doesn't dare to.*

La Chunga   Take it easy. What would you like? Feel at home. You're our blue-eyed boy. Just say the word.

Meche   We are here to please you. What do you fancy?

La Chunga   Do you want us to do a striptease, Monito?

Meche   Or dance stark naked, just for you?

El Mono (*covering his face, embarrassed*)   No! No! Please!

La Chunga (*pointing to the bed*)   Would you like to go to bed, the three of us, you in the middle?

Meche   Would you like us to be nice to° you till you can't stand it any more?

La Chunga   Would you like us to do some poses for you?

El Mono (*laughing, very nervous*)   Stop teasing me! It makes me feel ashamed. Please. (*He feels suddenly sad.*) You are the best, Chunga, Mechita. I'm sorry to be like this, but I'm not like you. I'm . . . I'm a shit.

La Chunga   Don't say that. It's not true.

Meche   A bit of a dimwit, maybe. But deep down you're a good boy, Monito.

El Mono   No. You're wrong. I'm a bad boy. The worst kind. It's no good you saying I'm not. The thing is you don't know. If I told you . . .

La Chunga   Tell us, then.

Meche   Is that what you want? A bit of sympathy?

El Mono   I don't want to force you. Only if you really want to . . .

La Chunga *makes him place his head in her lap.* **El Mono** *curls up like a frightened child.*

La Chunga   Come, rest here. Make yourself comfortable.

El Mono (*nerovusly, making a great effort*)   I didn't even know what I was doing to her. I was just a little kid, in short trousers.

La Chunga   Do you mean that little girl? Your neighbour Doña Jesusa's girl?

El Mono   I was a little kid. Do you think a kid knows what he's doing?

Meche   Of course not, Monito. Go on. I'll help you. You were watching and waiting for Doña Jesusa to go to the market, to her vegetable stall . . .

La Chunga   And when she went out, you got into her house and no one saw you. You got over the bamboo fence that faces the banana trees. Right?

El Mono   Yes. And the little girl was squatting there, milking the goat. She was squeezing its teats. Like this! And she didn't have any knickers. I swear she didn't.

Meche   We believe you. So you saw everything?

El Mono   More like she showed me everything, Mechita. Why didn't she have any knickers on? Why? So you could see her little thing, so she could show it to men.

La Chunga   Do you mean she led you on, Monito? In that case it wasn't your fault. She was asking for it, the shameless little trollop!

Meche   Is that what you are saying? That it was all her fault?

El Mono (*a little sadly*)   Well, no. I was a bit to blame as well. After all, I did sneak into Doña Jesusa's house, like a catburglar.

La Chunga   But not to steal, Monito.

El Mono   No. To see the girl, that's all.

Meche   You wanted to see her without her clothes, eh?

El Mono   I was only a kid, don't you see? I didn't realise. I didn't know the difference between good and bad.

La Chunga   But you had a knife, about this size, Mono. Don't you remember?

El Mono   I remember.

Meche   Didn't you feel sorry for the girl? Didn't you, when she smiled at you, thinking you were just being naughty?

El Mono (*disturbed*)   I *was* just being naughty. But she didn't have any knickers, Meche. She led me on. She . . .

La Chunga (*admonishing him, but not very harshly*)   The truth, Monito. The truth. She *was* wearing knickers. You made her take them off.

Meche   You threatened to kill her, Monito. Yes or no?

El Mono   Maybe I did. It's a long time ago. I can't remember.

La Chunga   Don't lie. You do remember. You grabbed her dress and you said to her: 'Get your knickers off.' And when she did, you saw what you wanted to see. Yes, Monito?

El Mono (*ashamed*)   Yes, Chunguita.

Meche   And you felt her too, didn't you? You felt her all over. Didn't you?

El Mono (*anguished*)   But I didn't force her, Meche. I swear to God I didn't force her. I didn't.

La Chunga   If you didn't force her, what was it you did? Isn't it the same thing?

El Mono (*laughing*)   How can it be the same? Don't be daft, Chunga.

He drops his voice, places a finger to his lips, 'Sh, sh', as though he is about to reveal a great secret.

I put it up her little arse. Don't you see? She was still all right where it really mattered. Not a scratch. Her husband could still break it on their wedding-night. It's a very important difference. Ask Father Garcia if you want. 'If the hymen is still intact, I absolve you. If not, there's only one thing to do: you'll have to marry la Jesusa's girl.' Well, I didn't, did I? . . . You women, your honour's in that bit of skin, in the hymen, and that's what you have to defend tooth and claw. But us men, now our honour's in our arse. And if a man has his arse tampered with, he's stuck with it, he's a queer for good and all.

La Chunga *and* **Meche** *look at him in amusement, silently. He is sad and sorry for himself. He sits up.*

Yes. You're right in what you're thinking. What I did to the girl was wicked. I managed to fool Father Garcia, but not you. I know that when I die God will punish me for it.

La Chunga   Why wait so long, Monito?

Meche   We can punish you now once and for all.

El Mono *takes off his belt and gives it to them. He bends down.*

El Mono   Go on. Make me clean. Let me pay for my sins. Don't take pity on me. Humiliate me. Chunga, Mechita.

La Chunga *and* **Meche** (*while they are beating him*)
Naughty boy! Spoilt brat! Wicked boy! Rotten, evil, vicious boy! Perverted creature!

El Mono *moans, cringing with the blows, sweating, experiencing a kind of enjoyment which ends in a great shudder.* **Meche** *and* **La Chunga** *sit and watch him. He straightens up, empty, sad, wipes his forehead, ties his belt, tidies himself up. Without looking at them, he goes out of the room and quietly takes his place at the table.*

La Chunga   Aren't you going to say goodbye, Monito? Aren't you going to thank us?

Meche   You can tell us more bad things, Monito. Whenever you feel like it.

Scene Eight: Two friends

After **El Mono** *has left the room,* **Meche** *and* **La Chunga**'s *manner changes, as if the previous scene had not occurred.*

La Chunga   Some hide it better than others. But just you scratch the surface, the scab comes away and you see the animal beneath.

Meche   Do you think all men are like that, Chunga? Are they all dirty pigs underneath?

La Chunga   All the ones I know are.

Meche   Do you think women are better?

La Chunga   At least what we've got between our legs doesn't turn us into filthy devils.

Meche (*touching her belly*)   Better to be a woman, then.

La Chunga   You aren't pregnant, are you?

Meche   I've missed for the last two months.

La Chunga   Have you been to see anyone?

Meche   I'm afraid they'll tell me I am.

La Chunga   Don't you want it?

Meche   Of course I do. But Josefino doesn't. If I'm pregnant, he'll make me have an abortion. He says no woman's going to tie him down with a kid.

La Chunga   I agree with him. What's the point of bringing more people into the world? What do you want a kid for? So when he grows up he'll be like that lot?

Meche   If everyone thought like that, the world would come to an end.

La Chunga   It can end tomorrow for all I care.

Pause.

Meche   Do you know something, Chunga? I don't think you're as bitter as you'd have me think you are.

La Chunga   I'm not trying to make you think anything.

Meche   Because if you were, I wouldn't be here. (*A mischievous gleam in her eye.*) You wouldn't have given Josefino three thousand for me to spend the night with you. Besides . . .

La Chunga   What?

Meche (*indicating the bed*)   Not long ago you were stroking me and saying nice things, like you were in heaven because of me, you were happy. Was it all lies?

La Chunga   No. It was true.

Meche   Life isn't so ugly then. It's got some good things too. (*She laughs.*) I'm glad I'm one of the good things life can give you. Can I ask you something?

La Chunga   If it's how many women have been here before you, don't bother. I'm not going to tell you.

Meche   No, it's not that. I'd like to know if you could fall for me, Chunga. Like a man for a woman. Could you love me?

La Chunga   I wouldn't fall for you or anyone else.

Meche   I don't believe you, Chunga. No one can live
without love. What would life be if you didn't love someone,
or someone didn't love you?

La Chunga   The woman who falls in love goes soft. She
lets herself be bossed around. (*She looks at* **Meche** *in silence for
a moment.*) At the moment you think it's great. But I'll talk to
you again when you've seen what Josefino does with your
love. I'll talk to you when you're in the whorehouse.

Meche   Why do you want to scare me all the time with
that?

La Chunga   Because I know how you'll end up. He's got
you in his clutches, he does what he wants with you already.
He'll start by letting one of the gang have you, one of these
nights when he's drunk. And he'll finish by persuading you
to go on the game. A little story about saving up to buy a
little house, go on a nice holiday, maybe get married.

Meche   When you tell me that, I don't know whether
your reasons are good or bad. Whether you want to help me
or just scare me.

La Chunga   I want to help.

Meche   But why? Are you as keen on me as that? You just
said you aren't. So why would you want to help me? You've
got everything. No one matters a damn to you.

La Chunga (*looks at her thoughtfully*)   You're right. I don't
know why I'm trying to advise you. Why should your life
matter to me?

Meche   Did you ever talk like this to any of Josefino's
other girls?

La Chunga   No.

She looks at **Meche**. *She takes her chin in one hand, forcing* **Meche**
to look at her directly, drawing her face close.

Maybe I feel sorrier for you, because you are prettier.
Another of life's injustices. If you didn't have such a nice

face, I probably wouldn't care less what Josefino did with you.

Meche   Sometimes I think you're a monster, Chunga.

La Chunga   That's because you won't face up to life. It's life that is the monster, not me.

Meche   Well if life's as you say it is, it's better to be like me. Not to think about what's going to happen. To live for today – what will be will be.

She looks unhappy, looking at her stomach.

La Chunga   At least you'll perform that miracle: Josefino born again.

Meche   You know it won't happen.

La Chunga   No, it won't.

Meche *leans against* **La Chunga,** *letting her head rest on her shoulder. But* **La Chunga** *doesn't hold her.*

Meche   I'd like to be strong like you, to stand up and defend myself. If I didn't have someone to take care of me, I don't know what I'd do.

La Chunga   Not a cripple, are you?

Meche   I can hardly read, Chunga. Where would I find work? I could only be a servant. Morning, afternoon and night, sweeping, washing, ironing the shit of Piura's well-to-do.

Pause.

La Chunga   If I'd known you were pregnant, I wouldn't have made love to you.

Meche   Does a pregnant girl put you off?

La Chunga   Yes. (*Pause.*) Did you like what we did or not?

Meche   Like? I don't know. I . . .

La Chunga   Tell me the truth.

Meche   I didn't at first. I wanted to laugh. I mean, you weren't a man. I thought it wasn't real, it was a game. I was trying hard not to laugh at first.

La Chunga   If you had laughed . . .

Meche   Would you have beaten me?

La Chunga   I probably would have.

Meche   And you say that what men have between their legs turns them into filthy beasts.

La Chunga   I must be a man, then.

Meche   Of course you aren't. You're a woman. And if you wanted to be, a good-looking woman.

La Chunga   I don't want to be good-looking. If I was, no one would respect me.

Meche   Are you angry because of what I said?

La Chunga   What? You trying not to laugh? No. I asked you to tell me the truth.

Meche   I want you to know something, Chunga. Although I'm not a lesbian . . . I mean . . . sorry . . . I mean I'm not like you . . . I really like you. I'd like us to be friends.

La Chunga   Don't be a fool. Get away from Piura. Don't you see you've one foot in the trap already? Get away from here before Josefino really has you in his clutches. As far as you can. You've still got time. (*She takes her face.*) I'll help you.

Meche   You mean it, Chunga?

La Chunga   Yes. (*She swiftly passes her hand across* **Meche**'s *face.*) I don't want to see you rotting away in the whorehouse, going from drunk to drunk. Go to Lima. Listen to me.

Meche   But I don't know anyone there. What would I do in Lima?

La Chunga   Learn to stand on your own two feet. But don't be stupid. Don't fall in love. Do that, it knocks you off course, and the woman who's knocked off course is finished. Let them fall in love with you, not you with them. Look for security, a better life than the one you've got. Always remember this: deep down, all men are like Josefino. If you get too fond of them, you are finished.

Meche   Don't say that, Chunga. When you speak like that, you remind me of him.

La Chunga   It must be because I'm like Josefino.

As if he had heard the sound of his name, **Josefino** *gets up from the table. He climbs the stairs.*

Scene Nine: The great pimp

Although **Meche** *is in the room and follows the conversation of the scene with interest,* **Josefino** *and* **La Chunga** *behave as if she were not there.*

Josefino   Hello, Chunga. (*He looks around, his eyes passing over* **Meche** *without seeing her.*) I've come for Meche.

La Chunga   She's gone.

Josefino   So soon? You could have kept her here for a bit. (*With a dirty laugh.*) Get your money's worth! (**La Chunga** *looks at him with the usual stern, scornful expression.*) So how did it go?

La Chunga   How did it go? What?

Josefino   Mechita. Was she worth it?

La Chunga   You've been drinking, haven't you? You stink from head to toe.

Josefino   What was I to do, Chunga, when you'd left me a widower? Tell me. How did Meche behave?

La Chunga   I shan't tell you. It wasn't part of the deal.

Josefino (*laughing*)   You're right. Next time I'll have it written in. (*Pause.*) Why don't you like me, Chunga? Don't lie to me, I know you've never liked me.

La Chunga   I won't lie to you. It's true. I've always thought you a nasty piece of work.

Josefino   I'm the opposite, then. I've always had a soft spot for you. I'm being serious, Chunga.

La Chunga (*laughing*)   Are you going to try to have me too? Come on, then. Show me how you coax those silly girls.

Josefino   No. I'm not trying to win you over. (*Undressing her mentally.*) It's not that I don't want to, honest. I fancy you as a woman. But I know when I can't get anywhere. I'd be wasting my time with you, you'd ignore me. I've never wasted my time with women.

La Chunga   Right. You can go, then.

Josefino   I'd like to talk to you first. A proposition. Business.

La Chunga   Business? You and me?

Josefino *sits on the bed, lights a cigarette. It is clear that he has thought for a long time about what he is going to say.*

Josefino   I don't want to be like I am for ever, Chunga. Just one of the lads. Fuck, I've got ambition. I want to have money, drink the best stuff, smoke cigars, wear three-piece suits of pure white linen. Own my own car, house, servants. Be able to travel. I want to be able to live like the whites in Piura, Chunga. That's what you want too, isn't it? It's why you work morning, afternoon and night, why you slog your guts out. Because you want a better life, which you can only have with money. We have to get together, Chunga. You and me together, we could do great things.

La Chunga   I know what you've got in mind.

Josefino   Even better.

La Chunga   The answer's no.

Josefino   What have you got against it? What's the difference between this bar and a brothel? I'll tell you what: here you earn peanuts and in a brothel millions. (*He gets up, walks around the room, pointing with his finger.*) I've got it all worked out, Chunga. We can start with four small rooms, there behind the kitchen where you put the rubbish. Just something simple, like a cane and a wicker job. I'll look after the girls. Guaranteed top class, of course. Down at the whorehouse they take fifty per cent from them. We'll take forty, so we can have whichever girl we want. Just a few at first. Quality, not quantity. I'll give the orders, you run the place. (*Full of enthusiasm.*) We'll get rich, Chunguita.

La Chunga   If I'd wanted to run a brothel, I'd have done it. What do I need you for?

Josefino   For the girls. I'll be everything you want. Don't you think I've proved my worth already? I'm the best, Chunga. I'll only get the best, girls who haven't worked before. Even a few virgins. You'll see. Fifteen, sixteen years old. That's what turns the customers on, Chunga. We'll get all the whites from Piura here, all of them willing to pay a fortune. Girls starting out, mint condition . . .

La Chunga   Like Meche?

Josefino   Yes, well, Meche's not such a novice any more . . . Maybe she'll be the star attraction. I swear I'll get girls as good as Meche, or even better, Chunga.

La Chunga   What if they don't want to work?

Josefino   I'll see to that. I may not know much else, but I do know how to teach a girl that what God's given her gives her a winning number in the lottery. I've made a fortune for the whorehouse taking girls there. And what the fuck for? For them to give me a few grubby coins? I've had enough. I'm going to be a capitalist too. What do you say, Chunguita?

La Chunga   I've told you. No.

Josefino   But why? Don't you trust me?

La Chunga   Of course I don't. The day after we went into business, you'd have your fingers in the till.

Josefino   I swear to God, Chunga. You'll handle all the money. I accept that. You'll be in charge of the girls' financial arrangements. You'll decide the percentages. I won't touch a cent. You'll have *carte blanche*. You'll make the decisions. What more do you want? Don't turn your back when fortune knocks at your door.

La Chunga   You'll never bring anyone any luck, Josefino. Least of all a woman. You are bad luck as far as women are concerned. For their sins they believe what you tell them.

Josefino   I didn't know you'd become a saint, Chunguita. I've never held a pistol to any woman's head. I convince them of one thing: in a single night in the whorehouse they can earn more than they would for six months' work in the market. True or false? Thanks to me, some of them live better than you or me.

La Chunga   It's not because I'm a saint I don't want to be your partner. I couldn't care less about the girls. If they are daft enough to listen to you, they deserve what they get.

Josefino   I don't like the way you are talking to me, Chunga. I've come here with a business proposition. And all you do is insult me. So, what if I get annoyed? Do you know what could happen if I got annoyed? Or do you think you are man enough to deal with me? (*As he speaks, he becomes more angry.*) The truth is, I'm up to here with your fucking airs, with the way you carry on, as if you own the bloody world. I've had enough! I'm going to teach you a lesson, put you in your place. You've been asking for it for a long time. No woman's going to look down on me, especially a bloody lesbian.

He draws his knife to threaten **La Chunga** *as if she were in front of him. But in reality she has moved alongside* **Meche**. *Both of them watch* **Josefino**, *who continues to speak to an invisible* **Chunga**.

Now then, lesbian. You are dead scared, aren't you? Pissing yourself, aren't you? Well, now you are going to see how I deal with cocky women. There's nothing I like more than a cocky woman. It really turns me on. Down on your knees, you! Quick about it if you don't want a face like a crossword. On your knees, I said. You think yourself important just because you run this pigsty? Just because you've got two pennies to rub together from overcharging us poor pricks who come here to drink your beer, and in spite of you being so unpleasant? Do you think I don't know who you are? Do you think the whole of Piura doesn't know you were born in the whorehouse? Amongst the tarts, the piss and all the good-for-nothings. No, don't move. Stay on your knees, or I'll cut you into little pieces. That's what you are, Chunga. A girl from the whorehouse, a whore's daughter, no mistake. So don't take on airs with me. I know where you come from. Now then, suck me off. Come on, you piece of shit, suck me off or you are dead. Obey your man, Chunga. Suck me. Slow and gentle. Learn to be my whore. *(For a few moments he mimes the scene, sweating, trembling, caressed by the invisible* **Chunga**.) Now, swallow it. It's a birthday present. *(He laughs, satisfied now, and even a little bored.)* They say it's good for the complexion . . . Were you scared then? Did you think I was going to kill you? How stupid can you get! I could never kill a woman: I'm a gentleman at heart, Chunguita. I respect the weaker sex. You see? It's just a game. It keeps me happy. I expect you've got your hang-ups too. You can tell me what they are when we get to know each other. I'll give you a good time. I'm not one of those that think women shouldn't enjoy themselves, and if you let them they'll make a fool of you. That's the sort of thing people like El Mono and José think. Not me though. I'm very fairminded. Why shouldn't a woman have her rights? Let's settle our differences, Chunguita. Don't be mean. Let's be friends. Bury the hatchet, eh? (**La Chunga** *has appeared* *again close to* **Josefino**.) What about our deal, then? We'll be rich, I promise.

La Chunga   We'd never be rich. Maybe we'd make more than I do now. But I'd be the loser. Sooner or later you'd make me feel you were stronger than me, like now. And if I disagreed, you'd get your knife out, or use your fists or feet on me. You'd be the one to gain. I'd rather die poor than get rich with you.

Josefino *goes to join the others at the table.*

Josefino   By God, women can be hard.

Scene Ten: End of the party

A long pause between **Meche** *and* **La Chunga** *while they watch* **Josefino** *descending the stairs and taking his place with the others.*

Meche   Tell me, Chunga, can I go now? It'll be light soon. It must be six o'clock.

La Chunga   Of course you can go. Wouldn't you prefer to sleep for a bit?

Meche   I'd rather go, if you don't mind.

They go down the stairs together and approach the door. They stop by the rocking-chair. The men have finished their beers and carry on playing, yawning, without seeing the women.

Meche (*hesitating*)   If you want me to come again, I mean, to spend the night . . .

La Chunga   Of course I'd like us to spend another night together.

Meche   No problem then. It doesn't bother me, Chunga.

La Chunga   Wait, let me finish. I'd like to, but I don't want to. And I don't want you to come here again.

Meche   But why not, Chunga? What have I done?

La Chunga *looks at her for a moment in silence and takes her face in her hand, as before.*

La Chunga   Because you are pretty. Because I like you and you've managed to make me feel sorry for you, for your way of life. For me that's as risky as falling in love, Meche. I've told you already. I mustn't be distracted. I'd lose the battle. So I don't want to see you here again.

Meche   I don't know what you mean, Chunga.

La Chunga   I know you don't. It doesn't matter.

Meche   Are you angry with me for something?

La Chunga   No. I'm not angry. (*She gives her a coin.*) Take it. It's a present. For you, not Josefino. Don't give it to him, and don't tell him I've given it to you.

Meche (*confused*)   No. I shan't tell him. (*She hides the money in her clothes.*) Taking your money makes me feel ashamed. It makes me feel like . . .

La Chunga   A whore? So, you'd better get used to it, for when you are working in the whorehouse. Anyway . . . do you know what you are going to do with your life? (**Meche** *is about to answer but* **La Chunga** *covers her mouth.*) No, don't tell me. I don't want to know. Whether you leave Piura or stay, it's your own affair. Don't tell me. I wanted to help you tonight but tomorrow's another day. You won't be here and it'll all be different. If you go and tell me where, and Josefino puts his knife here, I'll end up telling him everything. I've already told you I don't want to lose the battle. And if they kill me, there's no battle to lose. Go on, think about it, make up your mind and do what you think's best. But if you do go, don't tell me where, don't write, don't let me know where you are. Right?

Meche   All right, Chunga. I'll say goodbye, then.

La Chunga   Bye, Meche. Best of luck.

Meche *leaves.* **La Chunga** *sits in her rocking-chair. She takes up the position in which we saw her at the beginning of the play. We hear the men's voices beneath the smoke of their cigarettes. A long pause.*

La Chunga (*strongly*)   Now! Pay me and go. I'm closing.

El Mono   Only five minutes more, Chunga.

La Chunga   Not even a second more. Go. Now. I've told you. I'm tired.

Lituma (*getting up*)   I'm tired too. Anyway, they've skinned me.

José   Yes. Let's go. The night's gone flat.

El Mono   Let's sing our song first, lads.

El Mono, **José**, **Lituma** and **Josefino** (*their voices are flat, as at the end of a party*)
    We are unbeatable
    We don't want to work.
    We'd rather drink
    We'd rather shirk.
    We are unbeatable
    But closing-time's here
    It's goodnight to you
    And goodnight to her.'

They get up, go to the rocking-chair. **La Chunga** *gets up and takes the money for the drinks. She accompanies them to the door.*

José (*before going out, as if repeating a ritual*)   Will you tell me tomorrow what happened with Mechita, Chunga?

La Chunga (*shutting the door in his face*)   Go and ask your fucking mother!

Outside, the men laugh at the joke. **La Chunga** *secures the door with a crossbar. She puts out the oil-lamp that hangs above the gaming-table. Sleepily, she goes up to her room. Her movements suggest great weariness. She slumps on to the bed without even removing her shoes.*

La Chunga (*voiceover*)   Till tomorrow, Mechita.

Paper Flowers

by

Egon Wolff

This translation of *Paper Flowers* was first performed at Watermans Theatre, London, on 15 September 1993, with the following cast:

Eva   Linda Marlowe
Barracuda David Threlfall

Directed by Alan Gill
Designed by Anouk Emanuel
Lighting by Mark Berry

It was subsequently performed at Greenwich Playhouse by Workhouse Productions, opening on 10 July 2003 with the following cast:

Eva   Anna Kirke
Barracuda   Tim Molyneux
Tango dancers Tom Chadwick
                        Maria Guirao

Directed by Pauline Walsh-Burke
Designed by Ana Mestre
Lighting by Ben Pacey
Choreography by Peter Baldock

Scene One

The sitting room of a small suburban apartment, tastefully furnished, revealing a woman's touch. A comfortable, intimate room. There are two doors in addition to the front door: one leading to the bedroom, the other to the kitchen. One window. A canary in a cage. An easel with a half-completed painting. A box of oil paints. Ornaments made of straw: fish, animal heads, cockerels, et cetera.

The stage is empty. **Eva** *and the* **Barracuda** *enter. She is around forty, well-dressed, with studied elegance. He is about thirty, shabby, grubby, hair dishevelled, skinny, pale.* **Eva***, who opens the door, enters confidently. She walks towards the kitchen. The* **Barracuda** *stands in the doorway. He is holding two large paper bags. He shivers from head to toe. He looks at the room with a mixture of timidity and curiosity.*

Eva (*entering from the kitchen*)   Oh, do come in. Put them there, in the kitchen.

The **Barracuda** *steps forward with a kind of respectful caution, taking in everything. He puts the bags down in the middle of the room.*

Eva (*indicating the kitchen*)   No, not there. In the kitchen, next to the cooker.

The **Barracuda** *does as he is told. He returns without the bags.* **Eva** *has gone into the bedroom. She reappears combing her hair. She takes a note from her handbag, which has been left on a table, and gives it to him.*

Eva   This is for you . . . and thank you very much.

The **Barracuda** *doesn't take the note.*

Please, take it. Don't tell me you carried my shopping for nothing.

The **Barracuda** *stares at her.*

In that case . . . thank you. You've been most kind.

The **Barracuda** *continues to stare.*

Most kind, you had no need to. Thank you.

Barracuda (*his tone of voice impersonal, pained*)   I really fancy a cup of tea!

Eva (*a little taken aback*)   Tea?

Barracuda   You do have some?

Eva   Of course . . . but I don't have time. I have to prepare lunch and go out again. (*She offers him the note again.*) Take it. You can buy a cup of tea. There's a very nice place on the corner.

Barracuda   Wouldn't be the same, would it?

Eva (*curious, amused*)   No? Why ever not?

Barracuda   It just wouldn't

He continues to stare.

Eva   I see . . . but I really don't have time. Things to do, you see. Take it. You'll have to excuse me.

Barracuda   They are waiting for me . . . outside.

Eva   Waiting for you? Who?

Barracuda   Miguel, and his pal, Bird.

Eva   You mean the two who followed us? (*The* **Barracuda** *nods.*) So what do they want? Why would they wait for you?

Barracuda   They want to give me a going-over.

Eva   So what do you expect me to do? I suppose that's why you carried my shopping? So they wouldn't harm you. (*Annoyed.*) Here, take it. Please go. I've things to do.

Barracuda   They want to kill me.

Eva   That's your affair. You really have to go, at once.

Barracuda   I never thought you'd be so hard. You've got such a kind face.

Eva   It goes to show how wrong you can be.

Barracuda   Since I saw you last year . . . you were painting the flowers in the Botanical Gardens . . . I thought you was different.

Pause.

Eva   Botanical Gardens? You saw me there?

Barracuda   Behind the parrot cage. Painting some laurel bushes you was. (*He looks at her closely.*) You had a straw hat, with a green ribbon . . . and a headscarf with views of Venice.

Eva   You seem remarkably observant.

Barracuda   I do notice certain things.

Eva   And so you offered to carry my shopping . . . (*Disturbed.*) What is it you said you'd like? I don't suppose you've eaten today.

Barracuda   A cup of tea.

Eva   Perhaps you'd prefer a bowl of soup?

Barracuda   Whatever you like.

Eva   There's some soup left from last evening. I could warm it up.

Barracuda   If it's not too much trouble.

Eva   You'd best sit down while I see to it.

She goes into the kitchen. Sound of crockery. The **Barracuda** *hasn't moved, not an inch.* **Eva** *comes back from the kitchen.*

Eva   Why don't you sit down? You can't stand there all day.

Barracuda   Not in these clothes.

Eva   I doubt the furniture minds in the least.

The **Barracuda** *produces a newspaper from the inside pocket of his jacket, unfolds it carefully and lays it on one of the chairs. He sits on it.* **Eva** *smiles at his expression. She puts a chair against the kitchen door to stop it closing, so she can speak from the kitchen.*

Eva   The Botanical Gardens . . . do you go there often?

Barracuda   Now and again.

Eva   To look at the flowers?

Barracuda   To feed the monkeys peanuts.

Eva   You like monkeys? (*The* **Barracuda** *shrugs.*) I find them disgusting . . . quite revolting creatures . . . Looking for fleas in front of everyone . . . It's quite hideous.

Barracuda   They do what they have to.

Eva   So you have time for that?

Barracuda   For what?

Eva   The Botanical Gardens.

Barracuda   Make it, don't I?

Eva   I wish I had more time.

The **Barracuda** *is suddenly seized by cramps he cannot control. They affect his entire body. They distort his face. He has to hold the table to stop himself falling. Concerned that* **Eva** *shouldn't see him in this state, he turns his back towards the kitchen door and puts his arms between his legs.* **Eva** *has, however, seen him. Finally, he controls himself.*

Eva   How are things at the supermarket? Plenty of customers?

Barracuda   There's always someone wants their shopping carried.

Eva *enters from the kitchen with a tureen of soup and cutlery for both of them. She places everything on the table. The* **Barracuda** *gets to his feet.*

Eva   It's not very hot . . . I thought you'd prefer it . . . don't get up!

Barracuda   It's OK.

Eva   Please! Sit down . . . and help yourself!

The **Barracuda** *remains standing, begins to help himself to the soup.*

For goodness sake, please sit down.

She goes back to the kitchen and reappears with a hard-boiled egg, a tomato and a glass of milk. She places them on the table.

If you don't sit down, I shall refuse to serve you.

Barracuda   It's very kind of you . . . I mean inviting me to eat . . . and sit here next to you . . . where I don't belong.

Eva (*openly*)   I've told you already . . . it's not important.

Barracuda   I thought you was just saying that . . . to be nice. (*He sits down.*) Doesn't do to take advantage. (*Indicating her plate.*) On a diet, are you?

Eva (*laughing*)   Yes. Otherwise, I'd soon be like a ball. I put on weight so easily. A bread-roll and I'm two pounds heavier.

Barracuda   That's terrible.

Eva   I know. And such a nuisance.

Barracuda   Mario's the exact opposite.

Eva   And who is Mario?

Barracuda   He's a mate of mine. He eats some bread and he loses weight. He's nothing but skin and bone. He's a mind of his own, Mario. The doctors tell him to eat more. He tells them to bugger off. (*He looks at her with a blank, fixed expression.*) You shouldn't do that.

Eva   What shouldn't I do?

Barracuda   Skimp on your food. You might become ill. You might die.

Eva   Does that matter? Does it matter to anyone at all?

Barracuda   It matters to me.

They eat in silence for a moment, staring at their plates. The **Barracuda** *eats his soup, without raising his eyes. Then* **Eva** *gets up nervously.*

Eva (*half-laughing*)   So that's how you spend your time? I expect you go to the Botanical Gardens to see how a single woman spends her time, painting laurel bushes. (*She goes towards the kitchen, comes back with salt and a serviette.*) Is that how I appear to you? A single woman killing time? (*The* **Barracuda** *looks at her, doesn't reply.*) Come now, tell me the truth. What do you think I am?

Barracuda   A woman.

Eva   Yes, of course. But am I married or unmarried?

Barracuda   Married.

Eva (*flirtatiously curious*)   How can you tell?

Barracuda   By the way you cross your legs.

Eva (*laughing*)   How amusing! So how do single women cross their legs?

Barracuda (*expressionless*)   They never cross them.

Eva *laughs nervously.*

Eva   You really are amusing. (*A half-smile plays around her mouth.*) Tell me . . . do you always stare at people?

The **Barracuda** *immediately lowers his eyes. She is both moved and stimulated.*

Eva   You were right. I am married. Does that bother you? What if my husband arrived suddenly and found us together?

Barracuda (*quietly*)   He wouldn't think anything.

Eva (*flirting*)   How can you be sure?

Barracuda   You shouldn't take the piss out of people like me.

An embarrassed moment. The **Barracuda** *has another attack of the shakes which he barely controls.*

Eva (*not quite knowing what to do*)   Would you like more soup? You've hardly eaten a thing. (*The* **Barracuda** *indicates that he isn't bothered.*) A drink then? (*Pause.*) Would you like a drink, to help you relax?

The **Barracuda** *gestures vaguely.* **Eva** *goes to the kitchen and returns with a glass of wine, which he snatches from her hands and drinks greedily. He calms down.*

Eva   There, that's better.

Barracuda   What?

Eva   You seem much better . . . I didn't intend to cause offence. I wasn't laughing at you. It's just that . . . well . . . it seems so strange that you should remember me at all . . . out of all the others in the Botanical Gardens . . . There's an old man goes there to paint . . . I wonder if you noticed him . . . he wears a dark blue hat and walks with a stick . . . sometimes takes his dog with him . . . (*She laughs.*) One day he got quite annoyed about the kind of green I put into my paintings . . . He complained loudly that it wasn't correct. I never understood what he meant by that. So there he was, leaping around me waving his stick. I thought he'd demolish my easel. (*During this speech the* **Barracuda** *has been virtually doubled up.*) Is something wrong?

Barracuda   No.

Eva   So what is it?

Barracuda   It's just that after the shakes my stomach hurts.

Eva   Would you care for a sedative?

Barracuda   No thanks.

Eva   You prefer to drink. (*The* **Barracuda** *looks at her.*) I suppose that's why you have the shakes.

He doesn't reply. A moment of embarrassment. **Eva** *goes towards the kitchen.*

You'd better finish your drink. I really must go. I open the shop at two.

The **Barracuda** *helps himself to more soup.* **Eva** *comes back with some peaches. She places one in front of the* **Barracuda** *and eats her own.*

Peaches aren't what they used to be. I can't think what they do with them. When I was a child I often went with Mother and Father to a villa near a river. For a small charge they allowed us into the orchard to eat the fruit, including peaches . . . as much as we wanted. Now they *were* superb. Today, I suppose, they export the best and leave us to eat the rubbish. I remember how Mother and Father would sit at one of the tables beneath the trees, and Alfred and I – he's my brother – would go and play in one of the barns. We'd climb on to one of the balers. Alfred really loved playing the hero, he'd wave his handkerchief like some kind of flag and we'd pretend to board a ship. (*She laughs.*) He was the brave captain and I the wicked pirate. What times they were! And we were so happy!

Barracuda   If you throw me out, Miguel and Bird'll kill me.

Eva   So what can I do? Leave you here?

Barracuda   They are waiting for me, around the corner, behind the chemist's.

Eva *goes to the window and looks out, barely moving the curtain.*

Eva   So they are! They are looking in this direction. (*She turns towards him.*) Well, what's to be done? You can't stay here. (*More firmly.*) I've explained already. I have to go to the shop.

The **Barracuda** *begins to splutter, suddenly and in a great rush of words. The tone is uniform and pitiful, like a litany. At the end he suffers another attack of the shakes.*

Barracuda   Bird . . . he's got a butcher's hook inside his coat. A butcher's hook . . . he's been waiting all day to get me. I beat him at cards last night, you see . . . I won some money. He says I pulled a fast one. But I won fair and square! He came to the place where I stay to look for me, but I spotted him in time and got away along the river bank . . . All morning I was hidden in the bushes . . . and then I went to the supermarket . . . and but for you he'd have killed me! If it wasn't for you taking me in, I'd be dead! If it wasn't for you inviting me in, I'd be dead! And I don't want to die!

Eva   It's all right. It's all right. No one's going to harm you! (*Not knowing what to do.*) Perhaps we should call the police. They could arrest them. (*The* **Barracuda** *shakes his head.*) Ah, yes, of course. Honour amongst thieves, that kind of thing. (*The* **Barracuda** *is withdrawn into himself. He trembles. She thinks for a moment.*) I suppose I'll have to lock you in. (*The* **Barracuda** *looks at her.*) But, please understand. We've never met. Apart from the bolt, the front door's locked from the outside. I'll have to lock you in until I come back.

Barracuda   Yes.

Eva   I'll lock the other doors as well. You'll have to wait for me.

Barracuda   It makes sense.

Eva   You'll find some magazines . . . today's newspaper . . .

Barracuda   Thanks . . . (*He smiles for the first time, a broad, open smile that says nothing.*) It's as if it was all . . . like . . . ready, waiting for me . . . I mean, the magazines and everything . . . What more can anyone ask for? To ask for more would be . . . ungrateful . . . I mean . . .

Eva   Of course!

Eva *takes the plates. She goes to the bathroom and walks around combing her hair. The* **Barracuda** *takes a bite of the peach. He gets up and goes towards the birdcage.*

Barracuda   It's a pretty bird. What's his name?

Eva   Joey.

Barracuda   Joey, eh? (*Makes a fuss of him, giving him some peach.*) Ps, ps, ps, ps! Be better in the tree-tops, eh? You greedy little beggar! (*Gives him another bit.*) There . . . that's it! (**Eva** *closes the bathroom door. The* **Barracuda** *finds himself alone.*) You're a greedy little bastard, you are! (*His voice acquires a hard edge.*) Do you know I'm the wicked captain and you are the brave pirate? Do you know that, you little feathered fucker? (*He rattles the cage.*) Do you know that? That I'm the wicked captain and you are the brave pirate, you little bastard? (*As if hurt.*) We've never met! (*He shakes the cage.*) I'll have to lock you in! We've never met, you little son of a bitch! . . . I'll have to put a lock on you . . . (**Eva** *appears from the bathroom, ready to go out*) . . . Ps, ps, ps, ps! Come on, Joey!

Eva *switches on the radio.*

Eva   If you want, you can change the wavelength.

Barracuda   Thanks. (**Eva** *goes towards the door.*) Missus . . .

Eva (*turns*)   Yes?

Barracuda   I knew it. Every time I saw you, I knew you were what your eyes said you were . . .

Eva   I'll be back at six. (*Indicating the kitchen.*) If you want something, help yourself.

She goes out. Sound of the door being locked from the outside. The **Barracuda** *rattles the cage.*

Barracuda   Eat the bleeding peach! Eat shit, you bastard bird!

He shakes the cage.

Scene Two

The same afternoon, just after six o'clock. The **Barracuda** *is making a basket out of strips cut from folded newspapers. A paper bird hangs from the lamp, a kind of seagull hanging by a piece of string. On the floor a heap of scattered newspapers. Among them the* **Barracuda** *is on his knees. Dance music on the radio. Outside the sound of brakes and the slamming of a car door. The* **Barracuda** *goes to the window and looks through the curtain. He returns to his work. The sound of the door being unlocked.* **Eva** *enters. She holds a carrier bag from which the neck of a bottle protrudes.*

Eva (*nervous but seeming to be casual*)   You see? It's just gone six. (*She closes the door, sees the bird.*) What's this? Did you make it?

Barracuda   There's no one else been here.

Eva   It's really lovely. A true work of art . . . Is it a seagull?

Barracuda   What do you think?

Eva   Yes, of course. It's a seagull. It's beautiful.

Barracuda   That's what it is, then.

Eva   And what's this? A basket? (*The* **Barracuda** *nods.*) Wonderful! Where did you learn to make these things?

Barracuda   It's for you.

Eva   Which? The basket?

Barracuda   All of it.

Eva   Well . . . thank you.

Barracuda   I hope you don't mind . . .

Eva   Why ever should I mind?

Barracuda   I mean the papers . . . me making such a mess . . .

He begins to collect up all the papers. He folds them carefully.

Eva   Believe me, it doesn't matter . . . (*She goes towards the kitchen.*) Where did you learn to do it?

Barracuda   In this place. Worked for a bloke made things in wicker. Thick he was. Only made chairs . . . I can make flowers too.

Eva   Really?

Barracuda   Camelias.

Eva (*from the kitchen*)   Good heavens! You don't mean to say you washed up. (*The* **Barracuda** *doesn't reply.* **Eva** *appears from the kitchen.*) You shouldn't have. (*He shrugs.*) You seem to have cleaned the flat as well. It's far better than when I left.

Barracuda   Found this tin of furniture polish. Thought it could do with a bit of a rub.

Eva (*smiling*)   I daren't go into the bedroom. Who knows what I might find?

Barracuda   You won't find nothing. I wouldn't go there, without permission.

Eva *goes into the kitchen and appears with salami, cheese and some packs of cigarettes.*

Eva   You shouldn't think that you've been neglected either. I said to myself: 'The nights are cold. What better friend than a full stomach?' And so: a little Bologna sausage; a little pâté; some Gruyère cheese . . . specially recommended by the lady who owns the shop. She's a friend of mine.

The **Barracuda** *scarcely looks at what* **Eva** *has been showing him. He has finished collecting the newspapers into a neat bundle and begins* *to take them to the kitchen.* **Eva** *is standing in the way and there begins a brief game in which each gets in the other's way.*

Eva   What are you doing?

Barracuda   Putting them in the kitchen.

Eva   Leave them. It's perfectly all right.

Barracuda   They make the place untidy.

Eva (*nervous and a little impatiently*)   It doesn't matter . . . (*She smiles.*) Put them down . . . there! (*As she speaks, she has that brief, nervous smile which is peculiar to her, as if laughing to herself.*) I went into the shop rather quickly . . . to buy these things . . . without thinking of any excuse. I knew she'd ask, of course, and so she did: 'But who's it for, darling? It can't be all for you.' I didn't quite know what to say. I muttered something or other, started to panic, and then had rather a clever idea . . . 'It's for a picnic with some friends.' Imagine it! Me on a picnic! (*The* **Barracuda**, *once more on his knees, carefully smoothes out the newspapers.*) If I'd told the truth, who'd have believed it?

Barracuda   No one.

Eva   That's what I thought.

Barracuda   For people like me, all you need's a bowl of soup. (*Indicating the salami.*) Never dream of eating that sort of stuff.

Eva (*laughs nervously*)   Don't you like it?

Barracuda   What?

Eva   Salami? Cheese?

Barracuda   You always ask two things at once. I never know which to answer first.

Eva (*hesitant*)   What about salami then?

Barracuda   Turns my stomach over.

Eva   How can you not like it?

Barracuda   It's not that. It's my stomach not being used to it. If it's not rice soup or things like that, it acts up, you see. I remember once, the nuns of the convent gave me roast beef with mushrooms. I was sick for two whole days.

Eva   I didn't think. I shouldn't have bought it.

Barracuda (*looks at her with his characteristic expression, which tells her nothing*)   You and your friends can eat it on your picnic.

Eva   What friends? I have no friends.

Barracuda   That's really bad.

He goes back to his work.

Eva (*animated*)   Well, I ought to prepare a meal. (*She goes towards the kitchen.*) That's what my life is: eating and more eating, morning, noon and night. I sometimes think that life is nothing more than a permanent meal, with pauses in between to get bored again, and then it's more eating . . . Of course, there is some pleasure . . . like sprinkling sugar over it all . . .

While she is saying this, she has gone from the kitchen to the bedroom, put on and taken off a cardigan and bedroom slippers, and opened and shut cupboards, with the **Barracuda***'s imperturbable gaze always upon her.*

What silly things we do! Opening cupboards, shutting cupboards! Putting clothes on, taking them off! If we counted the hours we spend doing pointless things!

Eva *goes to the kitchen. We hear the sound of crockery. A glass falls and shatters.*

Damn! How stupid! What's wrong with me today?

She appears from the kitchen, wrapping a handkerchief around her finger. She goes towards the bedroom.

I've cut myself. Hardly a day passes without me using the first aid kit.

The **Barracuda** *gets up.*

Barracuda   Anything I can do?

Eva (*from the bedroom*)   I'm perfectly all right. I'm quite used to it. My fingers are nothing but cuts. I must have lost pints of blood. And it's not as if I do it deliberately. (*She appears from the bedroom.*) I mean, who would? (*She gives him a pair of scissors and a piece of gauze.*) Could you cut it here?

The **Barracuda** *cuts the gauze.*

Barracuda   You need some iodine.

Eva   Ah, yes.

Eva *goes to the bedroom and returns with a bottle of iodine which the* **Barracuda** *applies carefully and skilfully, placing the gauze on the cut and fixing the gauze with a plaster.* **Eva** *watches him as he does it. He tries to avoid all physical contact with her. She, in contrast, does not display the same reticence; rather, she has a kind of sympathetic curiosity in the face of his shyness. When he has finished, the* **Barracuda** *begins to tremble. He sits down, squeezing his arms between his knees as he often does.* **Eva** *goes to the kitchen and returns with a glass of wine which he drinks greedily. He calms down, coughs.*

Eva   Is that better? (*She looks at her bandaged finger.*) You've done it very neatly. Where did you learn?

Barracuda   In this place.

Eva   You seem to have learned a lot in that place. The only thing you didn't learn was how to talk . . . Are you always so sparing with words?

Barracuda   Where I come from they never want to listen.

Eva (*ironically*)   Believe me, it's exactly the same where I come from.

Barracuda   Put the cardigan on.

Eva   What?

Barracuda   Put the cardigan on . . . and the slippers.

Eva   I'm perfectly happy as I am.

Barracuda   You were going to put them on . . .

Eva   True . . . but now I'd rather not . . . Stop looking at me like that! (*She laughs nervously.*) Stop staring! Heavens above, you really do stare, you know. Do you always stare at people? (*The* **Barracuda** *looks down.*) You make someone feel completely . . . (*She goes towards the kitchen.*) Anyway, I want you to tell me where you learned to use your hands . . . I mean, with bandages and plaster. (*From the kitchen.*) You give the impression of being very experienced.

Barracuda   A sick sergeant taught me it.

Eva   You mean in the army?

Barracuda   In the hospital.

Eva   Were you a patient?

Barracuda   Sort of.

Eva   What was wrong?

Barracuda   Look, I can't talk . . . (**Eva** *appears from the kitchen.*) I can't talk to you like this . . . with you in the kitchen and me here, having to shout. I can't talk if I don't see someone's face. Don't get me wrong, but you don't relax enough.

Eva (*with keen curiosity*)   Whatever do you mean?

Barracuda   Well, you're always on the move . . . here, there, up, down . . . haven't stopped . . . Have you stopped to look at this basket?

Eva   Of course I have.

Barracuda   I mean, have you really looked?

Eva   Yes, I said I have.

Barracuda   Considered it?

Eva   Yes.

Barracuda   Do you like it?

Eva   Yes. I said so.

Barracuda   Why?

Eva (*lost*)   But it's just . . . a basket.

Barracuda   It's more than a basket.

An embarrassed pause.

Eva   Of course. You're right. Forgive me.. . . I told you
earlier: I'm like a machine . . . My way of life is to blame.

Barracuda   I could show you how I make flowers . . .
paper flowers.

Eva (*suddenly interested*)   Yes, I'd like that. Show me!

She squats next to him.

Barracuda (*taking a page of newspaper*)   You take a piece of
newspaper. You fold it from the corner, see? (*He folds it.*) But
not an ordinary piece of paper . . . it has to be one with lots
of print, or a big photograph, or lots of photographs without
any captions . . . see? So that the flower has some meaning,
a sense of continuity, a kind of beauty. (*As he works and speaks,
something happens to him, takes him over, absorbs him.*) For some
people, a newspaper's just a newspaper . . . a piece of useless
paper . . . for wrapping meat or blocking up holes . . . You
know the sort of person . . . easy to spot and always
superficial . . . But newspaper has so many things to say,
takes on the shapes you want to give it, folds easily, lets you
do what you want with it . . . don't take much room in your
pocket . . . keeps you company on winter nights . . . don't
cause you bother . . . lets you do what you want with it. (*The
flower is finished.*) There, finished. A camelia . . . (*He places it in*
Eva*'s hair.*) Just the thing for a lovely lady.

Eva   Who are you?

Barracuda   I can make carnations, and chrysanthemums
too, but you need a pair of scissors for that . . . it's much

more difficult . . . and scissors aren't easy to come by . . . not on winter nights on the river bank . . . (*His excitement continues to grow.*) I can make fish too, and butterflies. But that's more tricky because, when I make them, no one wants them . . . People only want fish in fish tanks, pretty and all lit up, and butterflies placed in little mahogany boxes . . . not made from stinking paper used to wrap the meat! Who wants dirty paper butterflies placed in little mahogany boxes? Who wants dirty flowers, made from dirty paper, dirtying their hair? (*He is breathing heavily.*) At least that's what the posh people say . . . the ones who decide what others should wear . . . who make the decisions . . . who tell me how I should shape the newspaper . . .

He coughs. Pause.

Eva   Who are you?

Barracuda   People call me 'Barracuda'.

Eva   I mean your real name.

Barracuda   Don't know. When you live on the streets you lose your name, like you drop it down a grating.

Eva   But you must have a name. I can't very well call you 'Barracuda'.

Barracuda (*expressionless*)   Why not?

Eva (*confused*)   Well . . . I suppose because . . .

Barracuda (*expressionless*)   It's a name from the other side of the tracks.

Eva   It's not your Christian name.

Barracuda   And you aren't from the other side of the tracks.

Eva (*with a certain defiance*)   Of course I'm not, if that's the way you want to put it. My friends and I use Christian names.

Barracuda   You said you didn't have no friends.

Eva   That was just a manner of speaking.

Barracuda   Well we aren't as good as you, you see, so we don't use Christian names. (*Smiling more calmly*.) My mother calls me Roberto.

Eva   That's better. I'll call you Roberto, then.

Barracuda   Beto.

Eva   Beto?

Barracuda   And bastard. Bastard before dinner, Beto after it. I had two mothers. One before, the other after.

Eva   You mean one died?

Barracuda   You could say that.

Eva gets up and, with an exaggerated vivacity, goes to one of the pieces of furniture, produces a pair of scissors and gives it to him.

Eva   So! We aren't on the river bank; we have a pair of scissors. Show me how you make chrysanthemums! Do you mind if I knit at the same time? I promised to make a top for a girl in my shop.

Eva sits close to him, with her wool and needles. Her attitude is that of a person who feels close to someone else; who feels at ease; who shows interest.

Eva   Show me.

Barracuda (*getting up*)   I ought to be on my way.

Eva (*it hadn't occurred to her*)   Oh, yes. Of course! But won't those men be there?

She gets up and goes to the window.

Barracuda   They are still waiting. I told you they wasn't messing about.

Eva   But what do they want? All you did was win some money at cards. Aren't you allowed to win?

Barracuda   Yes. But they make you pay for it.

Eva   I don't understand. How can they be so vindictive?

Barracuda   They see how dogs fight for a piece of meat.

Eva   You mean they'll attack you as soon as you leave?

Barracuda   They won't turn a hair.

Eva   Well, we can't have them doing that.

Barracuda   Would you like to see me make chrysanthemums?

Eva   You'll stay here until they've gone.

The **Barracuda** *begins to cut the paper. He does it with rising fury which is, at first, contained.*

Barracuda   You take a sheet of paper, and you cut it from the corners, see? (*He cuts.*) You make long cuts, along the print . . . until you've got strips of paper . . . as thin as you can make them . . . Till the original's no more than loads of strips . . . as if a dog had torn it to shreds . . . or a bird of prey . . . or a wild animal . . . like when, on the buses, someone rips the seats with a blade and leaves the mark of his rage and anger . . . like when in the army hospital your back is raw from all the lashes and the nurse puts iodine on it!

Eva   Beto . . . (*He looks at her.*) May I call you Beto? (*He looks at her, his eyes expressionless.*) Would you like to sleep here? For tonight? In the armchair? You can have some blankets . . . I really don't mind.

Barracuda   But you gave me cheese and salami, so then I'd be on my way.

Eva   But you can't go, Beto. Not yet.

Barracuda   If I stay here I'll have to . . . have a bath. Stands to reason.

Eva   Did I say you'd have to?

The **Barracuda** *laughs and looks at* **Eva** *to see if she is laughing.*

Barracuda (*laughing*)   No! But say it! 'I'd like you take a bath, Beto.'

Eva   It's as good as said.

Barracuda (*laughing*)   No. it's not the same. I want you to say it. I want to see how you say it: 'I'd like you take a bath, Beto . . . those dirty clothes, all that grime . . .' Say it!

Eva   All right, if you insist. 'I'd like you to take a bath, Beto!'

Barracuda (*suddenly serious*)   But . . . I can't take a bath in your bath . . . How could I even think of it?

Eva   Of course you can! Have I said you can't?

Barracuda   You haven't, no. But you wouldn't, would you? I get some funny ideas. Can't think how I could think of it. (*Suddenly.*) I'll show you how to make chrysanthemums.

Eva   But you've shown me already.

He stares at her.

Barracuda   You weren't paying attention.

Eva (*protesting*)   But I was.

Barracuda   Your eyes were fixed on your knitting.

Eva   All right, show me.

The **Barracuda** *takes another sheet of newspaper and begins to cut it as before.*

Barracuda   You take a sheet of paper, and you cut it from the corners. See? You make long cuts, along the print . . . until you've got strips of paper . . . as thin as you can make them . . . till the original's no more than loads of strips . . . (*His voice has become tense, the words squeezed from his mouth.*) Like when, on the buses, someone rips the seats with a blade . . .

Scene Three

Early the following morning. The **Barracuda** *is already up. He has had a bath and combed his hair. His clothes are folded on a chair. Next to them, his shoes. He is wearing one of* **Eva**'s *dressing gowns which is short and tight on him. He is going around the room with a brush and a duster. He draws back the curtains. He dusts the furniture. From the kitchen the sound of a kettle. He hums a tune as he dusts. The sunlight floods in. The straw ornaments have disappeared. Instead of them, hanging on the walls and from string stretched from wall to wall, are paper flowers and butterflies. A moment later . . .*

Eva (*from the bedroom*)   Good morning!

Barracuda   Morning!

Eva   Did you sleep well?

Barracuda   Perfect.

Eva   You're up awfully early.

Barracuda   It's a nice morning.

Eva   What are you doing?

Barracuda   A bit of cleaning.

Eva   But why?

The door of the bedroom is opened with a key from the inside. **Eva** *enters in her dressing gown, combing her hair.*

Eva   You shouldn't have.

When she sees the **Barracuda** *she cannot conceal her amusement or astonishment.*

Barracuda   I had a bath . . . Hope you don't mind.

Eva   No, no. why should I mind?

Barracuda   The soap had such a lovely smell . . . I think it must have gone to my head . . . didn't know what I was doing . . . Woke up. I was wearing this!

Eva   It's perfectly fine.

Barracuda   Said to myself: 'Barracuda, do something useful.' I looked outside and saw all the flowers and the swallows chasing each other, and said to myself: 'Barracuda, do something useful' . . . (*He laughs in his customary manner: a laugh which fills his entire face but says nothing.*) On a morning like this, even the rats down by the river like to take a walk. How do you like your egg?

Eva   Egg?

Barracuda   Egg.

Eva   But, Beto, there's . . .

Barracuda   Fried or boiled?

Eva (*thankfully resigned*)   Boiled.

Barracuda   I was right. It's boiling already. I hope you don't mind.

Eva   What?

Barracuda   Me using the eggs, without asking.

Eva   Why should I mind?

Barracuda   You said that yesterday . . .

Eva   What?

Barracuda   'Why should I mind?' Funny how we repeat things. (*While he is speaking, he is tidying his improvised bed. He folds the blankets carefully.* **Eva** *goes into the bathroom.*) Had a friend once, in this place I was working in, sawmill down south. He had a saying. 'I'm innocent', he used to say, morning, noon and night . . . never stopped. Must have been a kind of obsession, never gave him a moment's peace . . . 'I'm innocent . . . I'm innocent'. Drove us round the bend that did. One day a few of us got hold of him, hung him upside down to try to stop him . . . Not a chance . . . Even hanging upside down, 'I'm innocent, I'm innocent', he'd say. We never got to know what he was innocent of.

He must have thought he was innocent of something . . . gave him something to live for . . . Funny, sayings . . . Don't mean nothing half the time.

Eva *comes out of the bathroom, putting a ribbon in her hair.*

Eva   You seem very chatty this morning. Quite different from last evening. I'm glad to see it.

The **Barracuda** *shrugs his shoulders, lifts up the carpet, sweeps.*

Barracuda   Seeing the flowers cheered me up.

Eva *looks at him.*

Eva   It shows in your face. You look quite different.

Barracuda (*laughs happily*)   Think it must have been the bath . . .

Eva *notices the straw ornaments are no longer there.*

Eva   My ornaments!

Barracuda   What?

Eva   My straw ornaments! The donkey's head, the cockerel.

Barracuda   I put them in a cupboard, in the kitchen.

Eva (*surprised*)   Why?

Barracuda (*indicating the flowers*)   Thought these looked better.

Eva (*not knowing what so say*)   Well, yes, of course . . .

Barracuda   I suppose you don't mind?

Both (*together*)   No! Why should I mind?

The **Barracuda** *laughs. Then* **Eva** *laughs.*

Eva   In any case, I was thinking of getting rid of them. You've saved me the bother.

Barracuda   Didn't you like them, then?

Eva   I thought they were hideous.

Barracuda   Why's that? Didn't seem ugly to me.

Eva   So why did you throw them out?

Barracuda   Thought these looked better, that's all. Don't you agree?

Eva   Oh, yes. Of course I do.

Barracuda   Never run down what you've made yourself. You did make them, didn't you?

Eva   In a moment of madness.

Barracuda   Don't be hard on yourself. (*He hurries to the kitchen.*) The eggs must be ready. (*From the kitchen.*) By the way, I gave the canary some birdseed. Was that all right?

Eva (*goes to the cage, plays with the canary*)   Yes, fine!

Barracuda   I was going to give him some bread, then I thought; 'He's domesticated, he's not a sparrow, is he?'

Eva   Beto!

Barracuda   Yeah?

Eva   I heard voices . . . in the night.

Barracuda   Voices?

Eva   People talking. They seemed to be in the corridor. Did you hear anything?

Barracuda   People talking? No.

Eva   They seemed to be having an argument.

Barracuda   I slept like a log. Didn't hear a thing.

Eva   How strange! Then I heard a door slam. It must have been the neighbours. Italians, you know . . . part of some cabaret act. They come home at all hours . . . bring their friends with them. They seem to forget this is a place where people . . .

Barracuda   Keep themselves to themselves!

Eva   What?

Barracuda   The people here . . . keep themselves to themselves.

Eva   Well, yes . . . exactly. You always take the words right out of my mouth.

Barracuda   People who don't know how to live. You know what I think? They ought to live down there by the river . . . then they'd learn how *not* to live.

He emerges from the kitchen with a tray on which, neatly arranged, are two eggs in egg-cups, two cups, a teapot, a jug of milk, a butter dish, serviettes, as if this were a good class hotel. The **Barracuda** *has a folded, white cloth over his arm. He puts the tray down with style and elegance.*

Eva   You'll be telling me next you've worked in hotels!

Barracuda (*bowing*)   *Comment dites-vous, madam?*

Eva *laughs. The* **Barracuda** *remains serious.*

Barracuda   *Préférez-vous le beurre salé ou sans sel, madam?*

Eva *laughs.*

Eva   Who are you, Beto? Where did you learn all that? You're a man of many talents! Really!

Barracuda (*always serious*)   One has to do one's best.

They begin to eat the eggs.

Eva   But you have worked in hotels?

Barracuda   Yes.

Eva   As a waiter, I expect.

Barracuda (*his mouth full of egg*)   More as a thief. Great big, luxury hotel it was. Had to go in by the back door, so the guests wouldn't see me. I used to do the washing-up . . . not a contract job, of course. Only thing I'd get for free was a kick up the arse from the great fat git who ran the kitchen. Didn't half think himself important! (*Imitates him.*) 'Hey, you, get yourself behind that bloody sink. Get stuck in to those bloody plates' . . . five pence a plate he said he'd pay me. Nothing about me paying for the ones I broke. When it came to getting my wages, turned out I owed him five quid.

Eva   You owed him?

Barracuda   I owed him.

Eva   What about the French?

Barracuda   What about it?

Eva   Where did you learn it? In the hotel?

Barracuda   Had to stay there to pay what I owed. Fact is, I never paid it in the end. My debt got bigger, you see, day by day.

Eva   I see.

Barracuda   At the end of the week I was up to my neck. That's when I stole the computer . . .

Eva   Serve them right.

Barracuda   That's what I said. They didn't agree, unfortunately.

Eva   Was it there you learned French? Or in some other hotel?

Barracuda   Working for this bloke in San Andrés.

Eva   A Frenchman?

Barracuda   No, a Yugoslav . . . I can do shadows with my hands.

Eva   Shadows?

Barracuda   Yeah . . . (*Eating the last bit of egg.*) Dogs . . . foxes . . .

Eva   Why don't you show me?

The **Barracuda** *draws the curtains. He takes the lamp from the table, stands a newspaper in front of it.*

Barracuda   OK. What's this?

He projects a shape.

Eva   A dog!

Barracuda   And this?

Eva   A rabbit!

Barracuda   This?

Eva   A deer! . . . Let me try it. (*She attempts it.*) No. Isn't that hopeless! You'll have to show me.

Barracuda   Your index finger pointing up. Your thumb like this.

Eva (*holds out her hands*)   Do it for me. (*The* **Barracuda** *hesitates to take her hands.*) It's perfectly all right.

Barracuda (*taking her fingers carefully*)   You need to straighten this finger.

Eva   A deer! (*Full of enthusiasm.*) Let's try another one!

The **Barracuda** *is close to her. He continues to hold her hands. There is a short, awkward pause as their eyes meet. Finally the* **Barracuda**, *confused, goes to open the curtains. He switches off the lamp.*

Eva   Beto, you mustn't be so shy with me. (*She laughs.*) I shan't eat you. (*A little excited.*) After all, if both of us have spent the night here, we're entitled to a certain familiarity . . . don't you agree?

Barracuda   You are making fun of me!

Eva   Don't be silly, Bcto. All you did was touch my hand . . . I really don't mind.

Barracuda   People should learn to keep their distance.

Eva   What distance?

Barracuda (*indicating the dressing gown*)   It's because of this, isn't it? Because I'm clean! You've forgotten.

Eva   Forgotten what? (*He indicates his clothes.*) You *are* being silly! I've told you already . . . it's not important.

Barracuda   It's bound to be.

Eva   If you say so.

Barracuda   I think it's time I was on my way.

Eva   Well, I'm not asking you to leave.

The **Barracuda** *gets up and moves away from her, turning his back.*

Barracuda (*suspiciously*)   Why, then?

Eva   Why what?

Barracuda   Why do you want me to stay?

Eva   But I haven't asked you to stay. I only asked you not to leave.

Barracuda (*complaining*)   So who's to blame? Tell me.

Eva   Beto . . .

Barracuda   Who's to blame for being born, for what he is? I didn't ask my mother to be born!

Eva *gets up.*

Eva   Beto, for heaven's sake!

Barracuda   I'm nothing special, but I've got my pride!

Eva   Of course you have! Who says you haven't? (*She goes up to him, stands behind him.*) Beto! I'm not the woman you think I am. I'm a woman who needs a little affection. I may not seem to be . . . people think I'm confident . . . fulfilled . . . (*She smiles.*) But you've seen how I paint alone . . . Saturday afternoons, painting laurel bushes in the Botanical Gardens. Doesn't that seem strange to you?

Barracuda   I'll need new trousers. If I'm going to stay for a bit, I'll need new trousers. I can't wear *them* again. (**Eva** *looks at him without speaking*.) if I had to wear *them*, I couldn't stay.

Eva   That hadn't occurred to me.

Barracuda (*without looking at her*)   But it has now, right?

Eva   Well . . . perhaps.

Barracuda (*his tone changes, becomes anxious and intense, as it usually is*)   You see, if someone happened to call . . . if one of your friends suddenly dropped in . . . how could we explain . . . if they saw me wearing this . . . (*He indicates the dressing gown.*) Or those . . . (*He points to the trousers.*) And sitting in one of your chairs as if I was king of the castle? . . . They might even think I was some kind of dropout you'd taken pity on, to stop me kicking the bucket before my time was up, giving me a bite to eat . . . a bowl of soup, salami . . . Be no good, would it? Much too sad, all that. We wouldn't be able to stand it for long because we'd know . . . how could we not know? . . . the sad truth. There'd be between us a kind of moral poverty we couldn't disguise.

Eva   You think a pair of trousers will alter that?

Barracuda   We could pretend a bit, play a bit of a game. What do you think?

Eva   I think you need to put all that behind you, Beto. You brood on it too much.

The **Barracuda** *spins around. A broad smile illuminates his face.*

Barracuda   Blue trousers with a white stripe, a really thin white stripe. The sort of trousers I've always dreamed of.

Eva   We'll look for something you really like.

Barracuda (*like an overjoyed child*)   You mean it? You mean you'll go from shop to shop, looking for what I want?

Eva   Why not?

The **Barracuda** *takes her hands, raises them. He spins her round.*

Barracuda   You're an angel! You're a real angel!

Eva   Beto! For heaven's sake! (*She stops, worn out.*) To be quite honest, I don't really see the point of it. Things like that don't really matter, not to me.

Barracuda (*amused, teasing*)   Oh, yes, they do.

Eva   Of course they don't.

Barracuda (*wagging a finger*)   Oh, yes, they do! Yes, they do!

Eva   Why do you say that? What's so amusing?

The **Barracuda** *laughs as if he were telling an amusing and somewhat embarrassing story.*

Barracuda   The woman who brought you home last night . . . you didn't want her to come in.

Eva (*denying it strongly*)   No . . .

Barracuda   It's true. I could see she wanted to come up . . . and you were telling her it wasn't convenient, or something to that effect . . . It was really funny . . . you was thinking on your feet . . . looking for some way out . . . for a good excuse . . . I could tell by the way you were moving your arms . . .

Eva   It wasn't the reason.

Barracuda   Of course it was. But don't worry. I understand. If only you knew how I understand! (*Suddenly serious.*) What did you tell her?

Eva   All right . . . I told her . . .

Barracuda   You see? A pair of trousers will solve all that. You can tell her I'm your cousin . . . a distant cousin from out of town. What do you think? Maybe even an uncle. Which do you think she'd believe?

Pause.

Eva   You need to put all that behind you, Beto.

The **Barracuda** *lets his arms drop dispiritedly.*

Barracuda   Yeah. It comes from living by the river all
the time, lifting stones to see what's under them . . . moving
on all fours, looking for things, scratching about for
something to eat . . . in the end you see things from down
there . . . the entire world from the vantage point of your
little toe . . . and yourself even lower than that . . . even
lower than a toad . . . And in the end you become . . . I
don't know . . . sub something or other. (*Smiling again, but an
empty, meaningless smile.*) Subjected . . . subnormal . . .
subordinate . . . submerged . . . (*He stands before her, smiling
happily.*) A really thin white stripe! You'll buy me what I
really want?

Eva (*troubled*)   I'll do my best.

The **Barracuda** *kisses her hands.*

Barracuda   You're a real angel!

Eva *pours some coffee.*

Eva   If it helps, Beto, you should know I've become rather
fond of you. I think you have the makings of a . . .
worthwhile person.

Hearing this, the **Barracuda** *begins to tremble.* **Eva** *wishes to help
him but he gestures her away. He becomes calm again.*

Why are you so agitated?

The **Barracuda** *takes the newspaper and begins to make flowers.*

Drink your coffee.

Eva *goes to the kitchen.* There's no sugar. (*A sudden cry from the
kitchen.*) Oh, no!

Eva *reappears carrying the straw cockerel and donkey. Both hang
grotesquely, their necks broken.*

Why throw them in the rubbish bin? Why are their necks broken?

Barracuda   I couldn't fit them in.

Eva   You said you'd put them in a cupboard.

Barracuda   Couldn't get them in there neither. (*Protesting innocence.*) You said you hated them!

Eva   Well, yes . . .

Barracuda   I'll make another one, from newspaper. By the time you come back I'll have them finished . . . a cockerel and a donkey . . . how's that? . . . With strong, red feet and a golden crest. A great big powerful cock . . . all right?

Eva (*confused*)   Well, I . . .

Barracuda (*with his full, playful, empty smile*)   Don't mind me doing it, do you?

Both (*together*)   No, why should I mind?

The **Barracuda** *laughs loudly.* **Eva** *does the same. Both laugh wholeheartedly. The* **Barracuda** *laughs finally in an exaggerated, uncontrolled way, covering* **Eva**'s *laugh with his own.*

Scene Four

The same afternoon. The furniture has been rearranged. The door of the canary cage is open, the cage empty. The shade of the standard lamp has been removed. It now serves as a pot for three enormous paper flowers, held together with wire. In addition, there are flowers on the walls, on the lamp.

The **Barracuda** *is sprawled on the sofa, a woollen blanket around his legs, a bottle of whisky at his side. He is watching television. Because he has just washed his hair, he has a towel wrapped around his head. He is extremely happy and greatly entertained by the television. We cannot see the television screen, but we can hear the* *sound of shots and the war cries of Red Indians. The* **Barracuda** *becomes involved in the action. He imitates what he sees, hiding behind the sofa and shooting at the screen. He leaps on to the sofa, fires a shot. He is hit by a bullet. He dies dramatically in the middle of the living room. He is lying stretched out on the floor when the door opens and* **Eva** *enters. She is carrying some packages.*

Eva   Beto! (*The* **Barracuda** *doesn't move.*) Beto! What is it? (*She puts the packages on the floor, kneels at his side.*) What's happened? (*She touches him.*) Oh, God! (*She touches his face.*) Beto! (*She shakes him.*) Wake up! . . . Beto!

She looks around in panic, goes to the kitchen, comes running back with a glass of water. She holds his head and puts the glass to his mouth. He opens one eye.

Barracuda   Did you get the trousers?

Eva   Beto! What happened? You frightened me to death!

Barracuda   Blue, with a white stripe?

Eva *gives him a package which he opens eagerly, throwing away the paper.*

Eva   Why were you trying to trick me?

Barracuda (*with a cry of bewilderment*)   But these are grey!

Eva   I couldn't find the colour you really wanted.

Barracuda (*disappointed*)   I asked you to get me blue ones!

Eva   I'm afraid I didn't see any.

Barracuda (*shouting*)   Blue, with a white stripe. A really thin white stripe! You've brought me grey ones! What do you think I can do with these?

Eva   I looked everywhere . . . I . . .

Barracuda   You didn't. I saw three pairs in different shops only yesterday. (*He is holding the trousers at arm's length.*) What do you think I'll look like in these? What's Mario going to say if he sees me in these? He'll think I'm one of those show-offs, one of those Ministry blokes who can only warm their wives' beds! Those effeminate, soft-bellied gits! He'll say I look like one of them! (*He throws the trousers away.*) You can stuff *them*!

Eva *picks up the trousers. She is disappointed and wraps them up once more.*

Eva   I didn't think it was that important.

Barracuda   Of course you didn't. Anything's good enough for a tramp like me!

Eva   That's not what I thought.

An awkward pause. The **Barracuda** *switches off the television.*

Barracuda   I've changed the furniture. What do you think?

Eva (*not concentrating*)   Oh, yes . . . I like it.

Barracuda   Think it looks better?

Eva   Yes, much better.

Barracuda   Do you like the flowers?

Eva   Very pretty.

Barracuda   The canary got out.

Eva *turns to the cage.*

Eva   What? Joey? What happened?

Barracuda (*in the middle of the room, the picture of innocence*) Just opened the cage to give him some seed. Out he flew.

Eva   Where is he now?

Barracuda   Can't really say. (**Eva** *goes to the window, looks out.*) Just opened the cage to give him seed, shot straight out. Flew around for a bit in here, went into the bedroom, then the kitchen, then over my head again. Tried to catch him with a towel. Got one from the bathroom, did my best to pin him down. Thought I had him for a moment. That was when he landed on the picture frame. Positioned myself in front of him, waiting to throw the towel over his head . . . that's when I knew he didn't want to be caught . . . (**Eva** *turns to him.*) Had the upper hand, didn't I? How could I fail? Only had to throw the towel and he's mine. But that's when I knew he didn't want to be caught . . . Something about his attitude. Know what I mean?

Eva   So you let him go?

Barracuda   I wouldn't say that. There was a moment there I couldn't do a thing. That was when he took off again, did a circuit of the room and off he goes straight out of the window . . . towards the flowers . . . I know it's all my fault . . . He never took to me, that bird . . . Ever since I've been here, he'd never look me in the eye . . . as if he was scared . . . I think in the end he must have realised there wasn't room for both of us . . . (*He smiles his meaningless smile.*) They've got an instinct for these things, you know . . . Good thing really he went first, or I'd have had to leave . . . (**Eva** *goes into the bedroom.*) I'd given him a nickname . . . I called him 'The Pirate'. Funny name for a bird, of course, but I find it very suggestive. You have to be brave to live in a cage . . . 'The Pirate' . . . Poor bugger!

Pause.

Do you want me to leave?

Eva *appears, putting on a dressing gown over her clothes. She cannot resist smiling when she sees the* **Barracuda** *in the middle of the room: his arms at his sides, wrapped in the blanket, the towel around his head, his legs bare, full of guilt.*

Eva   Why would I want you to leave?

Barracuda   On account of the bird. Ever since I got here, I've been nothing but trouble.

Eva   Beto, you are just like a spoiled child.

Barracuda   How could I be so rude about them trousers! They were lovely really!

Eva (*taking his hand*)   Come along now. We need to have a little chat. I want you to be frank with me.

Barracuda   And you've been so kind and everything . . .

Eva *sits him down beside her on the sofa. She puts her finger to his lips.*

Eva   Now tell me, you spoiled boy, why were you in the Botanical Gardens the day you saw me painting?

Barracuda   Just . . . hanging about.

Eva   Come along, Beto. Tell the truth.

Barracuda   You're at it again, making fun of me!

Eva (*impatiently*)   Oh, Beto! Do stop it! We can't go on like this, you on the defensive, me not knowing what to make of you. I know you aren't what you seem to be or what you are trying to seem to be. All right, one little slip on life's 'slippery slope' . . . (*She seems amused by her use of the cliché.*) . . . that's what may have brought you here, but I know you aren't what you seem to be, or you don't appear to be what you are . . . But that's not important . . . You have to admit, I haven't asked you much about yourself . . . and if I had, you could hardly blame me. (*The* **Barracuda** *nods in agreement.*) So why not be a bit more open? Why can't we talks as equals?

Barracuda   What do you mean, 'equals'?

Eva   Precisely that, as equals.

Barracuda   And if I weren't what I seem to be, or didn't seem to be what I am, we wouldn't be able to talk like that, now would we? As equals?

Eva   Well . . . perhaps not.

Barracuda   Why not?

Eva   You'd soon be on the defensive again, putting obstacles in the way. (*She moves nearer.*) Anyway, be honest with me . . . What were you doing in the gardens?

Barracuda   Went to see the parrots.

Eva   Beto . . . the truth.

Barracuda   Mario sent me . . . I was looking for fag ends in front of the bandstand. We sell the tobacco to the local knocking-shop.

Eva   Why won't you tell me the truth?

Barracuda   And the deaf old girl, the one who sells papers outside the Parliament building . . . she asked me to get her a feather from the parrot's tail . . . to stick it in her hat . . .

Eva   You told me yesterday you remembered seeing me a year ago painting the laurel bushes in the Botanical Gardens. I was wearing my straw hat with the green ribbon. Now unless you were very observant and had a wonderful memory, no one would think you'd remember all that for all this time . . . if there weren't some special reason . . .

Barracuda   Special reason?

Eva   Some special inclination.

Barracuda   Inclination?

He has his back to her, distanced from her.

Eva   Oh, Beto, don't be so . . . shy!

The **Barracuda** *gets up.*

Barracuda   It's out of the question.

Eva (*still sitting*)   But why?

Barracuda   Where would it get us?

Eva   Does that matter to anyone? I wouldn't think that, leading the kind of life you lead, you ever worry about tomorrow. I very much doubt you worry about anything at all . . . So why now? Do you think that it bothers me?

Barracuda   It's different for you.

Eva   I can't think why.

Barracuda   Because you know things I don't know.

Eva   What 'things'?

Barracuda   That I'm not what I seem to be, or I don't seem to be what I am. As far as I'm concerned, I only know that I am what I seem to be and not what I don't seem to be. In other words, there's your fantasy and my reality, which is poorer, sadder and much more disappointing . . . (*Breathlessly.*) That's the advantage you've got, despite you saying I'm not bothered, I don't worry . . . What happens is a person worries so much about getting worried that, in the end, he stops worrying about it at all . . .

Eva   Beto . . . Look at me! (*The* **Barracuda** *turns but avoids looking at her.*) If you were the tramp you seem to be, we wouldn't be having this conversation. Can't you see that? All this would have ended much sooner, probably yesterday. You'd have finished your soup and gone. It's a sure thing you'd have bored me to death in no time at all. There's nothing more tedious than poor people moaning about their lot, don't you agree? I call them moaning minnies. (*The* **Barracuda** *agrees. He looks at the ground.* **Eva** *approaches him, takes his arm.*) As soon as I saw you, I knew who you were. I know your shyness comes from life having treated you badly. The things you've experienced have made you timid. But you must believe me when I say it makes no difference. I want no barriers between us, agreed? (*He agrees.*) Do you believe that I'm your friend? (*He believes.*) In that case . . .

Eva *awaits his response.*

Barracuda   In that case we can change the furniture.

Eva (*taken aback*)   Furniture. Why?

Barracuda   I can't stand it.

Eva   You can't stand it?

Barracuda   That's what I said.

Eva   I see . . . (*Lost for words.*) What's wrong with it?

Barracuda   It's got no class.

Eva   Class?

Barracuda   Or style. It's got no style. (*Irritated.*) Stuff like this, you can get it in any junk-shop. Makes you want to spew. It's got no imagination. It's got no magic. It's got no charm. (**Eva** *is completely startled.*) How long did you take to choose it?

Eva   I . . .

Barracuda   Five minutes, I expect. You went into the shop like someone going to buy a pound of carrots, picked the first piece of junk you happened to see, anything you could go to sleep on. Well, you made a big mistake. You need to be a poet to choose a piece of furniture, to look for the right quality. When the moment comes to make a choice, the part of the brain that deals with beauty has to be on constant alert. You are just like Fred, the bloke who lives across the river . . . off his rocker . . . couldn't care less where he puts his arse . . . some old paraffin-tin, a battered suitcase, a pair of shoes, the old geezer's chest, the poxy bloke who pinches railway-sleepers . . . he don't mind where! And he thinks that that's the answer! But choosing a piece of furniture's a ritual. (*He performs what he describes. As he does so, he becomes more excited, entirely concentrated on what he is saying. It is as if he is discussing the matter with some inner self, trying to convince him.*) You need to look underneath, you see, to check the supports . . . to see if they're pine or mahogany. There's always some smart-arse about who's looking to sell you a pig-in-a-poke and have you believe that softwood's hard . . . and then you run the risk of having your visitors spot your shortcomings. And then, again, you have to be sure your studs are properly fixed and your fringe is genuine satin, not second-rate stuff some son-of-a-bitch is trying to palm you off with . . . On top of that, it's very important, extremely important, to pay attention to shape, colour, design, to know your velvet from your brocade, to know what's what in terms of the latest fashion, if squares are out and rectangles in, if surfaces are concave or convex, if nails have been used instead of screws. Your visitors, you see, shouldn't simply flop down in an armchair . . . when they bend their knees they ought to find . . . they really ought to . . . that the shape of the chair is the shape of their buttocks . . . That's what you need to look for! That's what you need to take care about! It's very important. It's so important I'd go so far as to say it's absolutely crucial. (*He finishes, exhausted.*) A matter of life and death. That's what Fred could never understand. (*Pause.*) We need to get rid of this lot. It's our duty to our visitors.

Eva   Then we'll change everything. You can choose.

Barracuda   When?

Eva   Tomorrow?

Barracuda   Shan't be here tomorrow.

Eva   But you will. After today you'll be here as long as you like.

Barracuda   We'll need to go out.

Eva   What for?

Barracuda   To look at furniture.

Eva   So? We'll go out.

Barracuda   I've got nothing to wear.

Eva   I'll buy you a suit.

Barracuda   I'd like a grey one.

Eva   I thought you liked blue, with a white stripe.

Barracuda   That was the trousers. When it comes to a suit, I prefer grey . . . grey with tiny white flecks you can hardly see . . . you can . . .

Eva   Fine. It's agreed, then.

The **Barracuda** *looks askance at her, timidly, coldly.*

Barracuda   I need to know how we go about it.

Eva   Go about what?

Barracuda   How we walk down the street?

Eva   I don't follow.

Barracuda   Do I walk in front or walk behind?

Eva   Oh, not again! . . . If you wish, you can walk with me.

Barracuda   How far away? A foot? A yard? . . . And what will we say to the bloke in the shop? (**Eva** *looks at him without answering.*) Am I coming in or staying out? Who asks about suits? You or me? And what do we want a suit for? We need to invent a good excuse . . . We have to be convincing . . . None of your 'you see, it's like this', or, 'to be quite honest', or 'I know it sounds odd' . . . These blokes can be bloody suspicious . . . They suspect that you are what you aren't, or you aren't what you are as soon as they set eyes on you . . . Noses like bloodhounds . . . They see a bloke in rags and condemn him out of hand . . . He's a drunk, drug addict, pederast, pickpocket, pimp, exhibitionist, sodomite, child-murderer, queer, necrophile, shirt-lifter . . . as easy as putting a flower in your buttonhole. They see a bloke in rags and create a whole mythology. (*He turns to* **Eva**.) Know what I mean? We have to take the utmost care. (*His face is expressionless.*) What if we say I'm a tennis-player?

Eva   Why tennis especially?

Barracuda   Your husband used to play.

Eva   How do you know?

Barracuda (*indicates the bedroom*)   Saw his gear in the wardrobe. Think I could get away with it?

Eva   I think you'd get away with anything.

The **Barracuda**'s *expressionless smile.*

Barracuda   What about a gigolo?

He laughs. **Eva** *laughs too – a rather forced laugh.*

Eva   Oh, Barracuda, you really are the limit! Such a dark sense of humour . . . quite beyond me, I'm afraid. But I do admit I find you fascinating. (*She approaches him.*) You'll sleep on the sofa again tonight, but I shan't lock my bedroom door . . . You see? I trust you. (*The* **Barracuda** *takes her hands.*) If you feel lonely, don't hesitate to call me. I'm quite a light sleeper. (*Very close to him.*) Though I doubt you feel drawn to single women of more than forty who paint because they've nothing better to do, or for old time's sake keep a man's clothes long after he's gone . . . A single woman who can't even choose the right furniture.

Barracuda (*tense*)   I'll have to take another bath.

Eva *rests her head on his chest.*

Eva   Oh, Beto! You have to learn to relax. (*Pause.*) It's like resting my head on a rock. How life must have made you suffer!

Barracuda   *Comment dites-vous, madame?*

Eva (*looks at him, kisses him on the cheek*)   Oh, my love!

The **Barracuda** *looks straight ahead. He is a rock, a sphinx.*

Barracuda   You have to choose exactly the right words to make your meaning clear. A process of careful selection in which the soul becomes the guiding hand . . . in which the will can play no part. You have to believe in the beauty of your words, you have to give yourself one hundred per cent to them, cos if you don't and speak them carelessly, they come out false, and neither you nor anyone else will find them in the least convincing. What really matters is to say what you mean without saying it, so that others are to blame for deceiving themselves. It's the only way to be happy.

Eva   Oh, God!

The **Barracuda** *begins to make shapes with his hands, projecting them on the wall in front of him.*

Barracuda   A rabbit, see? . . . A bat . . . A kid . . . A frightened kid. (*He looks at her.*) Have you got an axe?

Eva   Yes.

Barracuda   I need a handsaw . . . and a hammer.

Eva   Yes, my husband had some tools.

Barracuda   Get them for me. Tonight I'll make some furniture.

Eva   You mean here?

Barracuda   Wherever.

Eva   They're in the kitchen. (**Eva** *goes to the kitchen. We hear her cry out.*) Joey! Joey! (*She reappears, dangling the dead canary.*) Who did this?

Barracuda (*downcast, suddenly like a child found out*)   I told you, didn't I? I was trying to catch him, but he wouldn't let me. He didn't like me from the start. He wouldn't look me in the eye. I chased him from room to room, begged him, pleaded with him to let me catch him . . . He wouldn't listen . . . (*Pause.*) In the end, he couldn't fly no more . . . he was far too buggered up to get my meaning . . . Kicked the bucket before I had a chance to explain . . . (*Pause.*) I could have learned to love that bird. (*Sobs.*) I could have really loved him . . . If only he'd let me! (*Looking at* **Eva**.) Poor little Joey! Poor Joey!

Scene Five

The following morning. On the radio 'The Waltz of the Dragonflies'. The **Barracuda**, *dressed in tennis gear, is kneeling in the middle of the sitting room nailing together a rough chair, or what appears to be a chair, from the remnants of the broken sofa. All that remains of this is a pile of stuffing and feathers, springs and ripped fabric. The wooden*

*items of furniture have been broken too, as if some bird of prey has been
at work on them. The pictures have also gone. In their place are
newspaper pages. There are paper flowers elsewhere. They are larger
than previously, less well made, approximations to flowers, made from
whole sheets of newspaper, rumpled, their stems tied with wire. The*
Barracuda *sings happily as he works. A moment later* **Eva** *enters,
dressed in a robe. She stands in the doorway, observing the*
Barracuda.

Eva   I heard you working the whole night long . . . as if a
giant mouse had settled here. (*She looks around the room.*) No
one could say you've wasted any time.

Barracuda   What do you think?

Eva   It's excellent.

Barracuda   I felt the urge, you see, and when I feel the
urge, it's just as if I'm seeing double . . . I see one thing that
needs doing, and straight away there's something else . . .
and when I start on that, another job needs my attention . . .
It's an ongoing thing . . . Mario won't believe that I'm a
carpenter.

Eva   He should come and take a look at this.

Barracuda   He says I'm only good at breaking things . . .
taking things apart. And to be a carpenter . . . a real
carpenter . . . to do it properly . . . do you follow?

Eva   Of course.

Barracuda   He says that I'm a washout. 'You're a
vandal,' he says, 'a complete hooligan.' He's always saying
that . . . maybe because he's only seen me doing this: putting
bits and pieces together, like a kind of jigsaw. Know what I
mean?

Eva (*going to sit in the one remaining chair*)   It must be on
account of that.

Barracuda   That's the trouble with Mario. He can only see things '*a posteriori*', never '*a priori*' . . . He ought to be here now to take a look at this.

Eva   Oh, definitely.

Barracuda   Make him shut his gob this would! (*Without waiting for her to reply, he picks up the chair he has just finished, holding it triumphantly aloft.*) Louis the fifteenth! What do you think?

Eva   Absolutely!

Barracuda   Maybe Louis the sixteenth.

Eva   No, definitely the fifteenth!

Barracuda   Why?

Eva   Well, because . . .

Barracuda   Yeah?

Eva   Because you say so . . .

For a moment a flash of anger in the **Barracuda***'s eyes.*

Barracuda   I think you are taking the piss.

Eva   Of course I'm not . . . I . . .

Barracuda   I can't stand soft-soaping people.

Eva   But I wasn't making fun. In fact, rather than Louis the fifteenth, I'd say it's Restoration.

Barracuda   Oh, yeah. (*The notion pleases him. He laughs.*) Restoration! That's good, that is! Restoration. I hadn't thought of that. (*Still laughing.*) That's what I like about you! You've got a sense of humour.

Eva (*laughing too*)   Do you think so?

Barracuda   Course you have. Ever since I got here. I mean, I've wrecked the furniture, let the canary out, filled the place with bloody horrible flowers . . . and there you are, taking it all in your stride . . . seeing the funny side of things.

Eva   What else could I do?

Barracuda . You mean the force of circumstance?

Eva   I'd say destiny.

The **Barracuda** *is suddenly serious.*

Barracuda   Nah! Destiny's more your cirrhosis of the liver or your lungs destroyed through too much beer and fags. Don't *you* think it's anything else! Remember me being here is strictly down to a bowl of soup . . .

He shows her the chair on which he is now working.

What do you think?

Eva   Beto . . . I left my door unlocked last night. You didn't come. (*The* **Barracuda** *concentrates on his work.*) I waited for you. (*Pause. Smiles uncertainly.*) I'd like you to know I wore a special nightdress. The nightdress I wore for my first night of love. (*She laughs.*) Afterwards, my husband insisted I wear it on our wedding anniversaries. It's full-length, blue, with two roses at the neckline . . . and it still has the scent of the pine trees at San Estéban . . . At least my husband thought so . . . He thought it had kept the scent of our first night beneath the pines at San Estéban . . . the sound of the waves breaking . . . almost over our feet . . . and the moon . . . the eternal moon (*She smiles.*) . . . like a close friend, watching us make love. (*She waits.*) Beto, do you think me capable of that? Of a night of love beneath the pine trees, with the moon as the only witness and my blue nightdress as a pillow? (*She raises her hand to her forehead.*) You don't believe me, do you? That's what makes you so unfair, that you can't believe it was possible . . . or that it still is . . . You can't believe it is still possible . . . (*He carries on working.*) . . . can you? You can't believe it . . . (*A vague, fleeting gesture, an uncertain smile.*) That someone like me, a single woman, could set aside her shame and open her arms to love with only the scent of the pines and the watching moon as witnesses . . . (*Looks at him.*) Answer me! . . . You aren't listening! (*She goes to the radio and nervously switches it off.*) Don't you believe me?

The **Barracuda** *goes to the radio and switches it on again.*

Barracuda   When I'm trying to work, I like some serious music.

Eva *is about to switch the radio off again but is stopped from doing so by the* **Barracuda**'*s cold, menacing, harsh voice.*

Barracuda   Don't you even think of it. I'm warning you. You'd better not!

Eva (*defiantly*)   And if I do?

Barracuda   I'll smash it to bits! Believe me, I will! I'll smash it to pieces!

He goes back to the chair. **Eva** *watches him horrified. Suddenly, his expression changes, becomes more relaxed, his old smile returns.*

Barracuda   Turn if off if you want. I mean, it *is* your house. The things I come out with . . . You mustn't take it too seriously.

Eva *goes to the kitchen. A moment later the sound of a glass breaking and* **Eva**'*s cry of pain and annoyance. The* **Barracuda** *has finished the chair. He raises it aloft.*

Barracuda   That's it, then! Finished! What would I give for Mario to see it! Shut his trap, this would! Good supports, fixed together properly! Solid back to it! Good lines! A quality piece of furniture! (*He goes towards the kitchen, speaks to* **Eva**.) That's what I used to say to Fred. 'The trouble with us,' I'd say to him, 'is that we've got no taste. All we do is complain . . . We always start from the premise that we can't afford the things we fancy . . . We spend our time being . . .' What was it you said yesterday?

Eva   Yesterday?

Barracuda   Yeah. I can't think how you put it.

Eva   When, yesterday?

Barracuda   You was saying that poor people bore you
. . . you said they was . . . what was the word you used?

Eva   Moaning minnies!

Barracuda   That's it . . . moaning minnies! That's all we
ever were. 'Fred,' I'd say, 'we are nothing but moaning
minnies.' Yeah, it's a nice expression! 'That's all we are,
Fred . . . nothing but moaning minnies . . . when the truth of
the matter is, we've got no taste. . . . So how can we ever
aspire to things if, from the start, we've got no taste? Fred,'
I'd say to him, 'if we limit ourselves to scratching about for
odds and ends, to rooting about in litter bins, to turning up
worthless bits of junk . . . you know. (*With scorn.*) Some piece
of crap you'd have to pay to get rid of . . . (*Miming.*) Making
ourselves into a ball . . . looking into ourselves . . . protecting
a few poxy coins from prying eyes . . . scratching our
pennies together . . . counting them like bleedin' misers . . .
how can we hope to fill our lives with beauty, Fred? . . .
How can we ever get out of the shit, you stupid bastard?' . . .
And then I'd say to him:

'If you don't have taste, your life's a waste;
If you can't hope to buy, you'd just as well die.'

Came out in verse it did, just like that. (*He puts the chair in the
kitchen.*) What do you think?

Eva   It's good.

Barracuda   You don't sound too convinced.

Eva   Oh, Beto, not all that again . . .

Barracuda   So what do you think?

Eva (*resigned*)   It's good.

Barracuda   How good?

Eva   Very good.

Barracuda   Better than the chair like it used to be?

Eva   Much.

Barracuda   How much?

Eva   Very much.

Barracuda   Why?

Eva   Because you made it.

The **Barracuda** *cries out like a wounded animal. He then draws into himself, begins to shake.*

Barracuda   That's not what I want. I want the truth. I don't want pity. I want the pure, entire, absolute truth! I want you to tell me: 'I can't stand your chair. It's the work of a stinking bloke who's off his rocker, whose hatred of things has left him stripped of any feeling for beauty . . . !'

Eva *enters, dissolving a soluble tablet in a glass. She drinks it.*

Eva   Why would I say that if I don't believe it?

Barracuda   You *do* believe it!

Eva   But I don't!

Barracuda   You're only saying that to cover up what's going on in there . . . inside your head.

Eva   I . . .

Barracuda   Out of pity!

Eva   For you?

Barracuda   Compassion!

Eva   Why would I feel compassion?

Barracuda   Out of feeling sorry! I know the signs in a person's voice . . . in every inflection of the voice . . . It's the voice of the person who looks down when he gives some money to a beggar, not the voice of the beggar who reaches up to take it . . . Let's hear you say: 'I really like your chair.'

Eva   I really like you chair.

Barracuda   No, no! you have to be more positive: 'I really like your chair.'

Eva   I really like your chair.

Barracuda   No! It has to be stronger altogether. You have to emphasise 'really like'. 'I *really like* your chair.'

Eva   I *really like* your chair.

The **Barracuda** *cries out in triumph.*

Barracuda   You see? The inflection in your voice! The way it trembles, the way it shakes with emotion . . . just a bit, but enough to show that what you feel is pity.

Eva (*wearily*)   It isn't true, Beto!

The **Barracuda** *shakes the chair.*

Barracuda   It's a bloody mess! (*Looking at the chair.*) It's got no style. It's been thrown together, not been planned, the joints are loose, the back's coming off . . . (*He begins to pull it to pieces.*) Nothing fits . . . the arms are useless . . . (*Pulls bits off systematically.*) It's a piece of shit . . . a load of rubbish . . . worthless . . . primitive . . . a waste of time . . . a pig-in-a-poke . . . a botched up job . . . the work of a bleedin' amateur . . . (*He scatters the remaining bits across the room.*) It ought to be on the rubbish dump down by the river, not in a class apartment in the city . . . (*He is finished.*) The end of what I dreamed of. (*He looks at* **Eva**.) But you should have said it yourself.

Eva (*as naturally as possible*)   I couldn't say what I didn't believe.

Barracuda   But can't you see it's driven a wedge between us? A great big gap that can't be closed again? (*He becomes declamatory, impersonal, sententious.*) Pity's a broken suspension bridge . . . it joins two people, one of them angry, one of them happy, like a spitting and a purring cat. (*He smiles his expressionless smile.*) What do you think of my metaphor?

Eva   For heaven's sake, Beto! What am I supposed to
think? (*He looks at her, full of despair.*) I never know how to take
you. Since you arrived, I've done my best to be nice to you.
I've tried to make you feel welcome here, but you persist in
. . . avoiding me . . . (*During the whole of her speech, the*
Barracuda *stands in the centre of the room. As she speaks, he
assumes the hopeless air of a guilty child about to be reprimanded for
something that can't be put right.*) I try to be honest, you tell me
I'm lying. I try to remove from between us whatever
reminds you of your poor background, you throw it in my
face . . . (*The* **Barracuda** *begins to tremble. He is the lonely child
who is cold and afraid, the epitome of the hungry, abandoned, cold,
homeless child.*) I'm not the well-to-do, cold, superficial
woman you appear to think I am . . . I'm a very lonely
woman who needs love and affection . . . I offer you my
love, Beto! (*She goes to him, takes his face in her hand. His whole
body trembles. He cannot control it.*) Try to be calm! Relax! I'm
here, with you . . . I'm here to help you . . . to give you the
warmth and the love you need. (*The* **Barracuda** *looks ahead
into an empty space.*) Beto! Look at me! I'm here! I love you!
Do you hear? I love you! Beto! Look at me! Beto! (*She shakes
him.*) Look at me! For God's sake! (*She shakes him more
violently.*) I'm speaking to you. Listen to me! (*She shakes him.*)
Listen to me! Look at me!

*No response. She slumps to the floor at his feet. He stops trembling.
Long pause. The music can be heard in the background.*

Barracuda   So what do you think of the outfit?

He says this without looking at her, simply staring straight ahead.

Eva (*crying out*)   You don't want help from anyone. You are
far too proud! Too proud to let anyone help! (**Eva** *gets up.
She is very angry.*) You won't let anyone near your precious
person! All right, I'll tell you my opinion of your outfit. (*She
moves away from him. She picks up paper flowers and other paper
objects and begins to throw them as she speaks.*) You know what
you look like? A puppet! A silly, deformed puppet! You've
got no chest. You've got no shoulders to speak of. You don't

have the build for a tennis outfit! You've got no right to put it on! (*She waits for his reaction, which doesn't arrive.*) You know what you need to wear such clothes? You need some muscles . . . strong and flexible muscles. Firm and decisive movements! . . . Not your twisted, half-starved frame . . . It's much more suited to rags! (*She waits again for a reaction. She approaches him, goes up to his face.*) You don't have a back! You have a hump! . . . (*She begins to sob, sinks to his feet. Her voice can barely be heard.*) You don't have muscles . . . you're nothing but skin and bone!

Barracuda (*distant, very quietly*)   And then, out of the bushes, a tiny bird appeared. For a moment it flew over the green leaves . . . Over the landscape full of light . . . Fly, little pirate, I said to it. (**Eva** *covers her ears.*) Fly, little bird! (*The* **Barracuda** *looks at her with a smile that also suggest pity. He sits beside her, becomes sententious.*) Love is truce between two states of exhaustion . . . Love is broken teeth in a hungry mouth . . . What do you think of my metaphor?

Eva (*tears in her eyes*)   I want you to leave. (*The* **Barracuda** *looks at her, puzzled.*) I can't go on playing this game.

Barracuda (*genuinely downcast*)   You're chucking me out?

Eva   Yes, yes! I am!

Barracuda   What'll I do?

Eva   I don't care. Just go!

Barracuda   It's exactly what I said to Mario: 'These people with money,' I said, 'you think you're on to a good thing . . . something comes up, and it's sweet Fanny Adams.' 'She'll be different,' he says, 'she's all on her own.' (**Eva** *looks at him, amazed.*) He was wrong, wasn't he?

Eva   You mean you discussed me with someone else?

Barracuda   But I'm asking myself, where would it have got us anyway . . . where would all your pleasantries have got us, eh? (*He looks at her.*) To feel love, you have to sweat . . . I saw this monkey in a circus once. They'd put his

girlfriend in a different cage and he wanted to get to her.
Must have been one in the afternoon when he started
trying. Kept on at it the whole night long till his chest was
covered in blood and his teeth broken from smashing
himself against the bars. They made it in the end, of course,
when he was dead and they let her in to see his corpse . . .
Touching, isn't it . . . love? (*He feels the need to talk. He sits at*
Eva*'s feet, crossing his legs like some Hindu.*) As long as love
exists, that is! There was this bloke, some saint or other, he
used to deny that it does exist, though he's even stopped
doing that now . . . he sits on the edge of a bridge, looking
into the water. You speak to him, not a bleedin' word. You
give him a poke, no reaction. You shout at him, he doesn't
move . . . Lost interest you see, in everything. He's got to the
point of turning his back on life, where he sees no sense in
struggling . . . They say a pigeon made its nest in his hat and
he didn't even notice . . . It's a story, of course, but it makes
the point . . . Don't you think so?

Eva   Didn't you hear what I said?

Barracuda   What?

Eva   I want you to leave!

Barracuda   Do you really think you do? Have we got to
the point of spiritual emptiness where the fight's no longer
possible?

Eva *gets up, cries out and runs to the bedroom, locking herself in. The*
Barracuda *watches her as she goes with a mixture of amusement*
and amazement.

Do you really think so, Pirate? That we've reached that
point of complete spiritual nothingness where love's no
longer possible?

He goes up to the cage, begins to speak to it, hits it, amuses himself
with it. The cage almost hits the ceiling. His blows become more
violent. He is like someone conducting an interview, making fun of a
series of clichés.

What's your opinion, sunshine? Don't you agree that the
human spirit, lacking all consolation, sinks into a terrible
state of spiritual prostration, where mutual confidence
ceases to exist? Don't you agree, Miss Sunshine? (*With a
savage blow.*) Don't you agree, you bastard bird? . . . What do
you say? You agree with me, you son-of-a-bitch? . . . Now
you flying off like that, without so much as a 'by your leave',
now that was a piece of shit if ever there was! Well, wasn't
it? Wasn't it?

The cage is smashed against the wall.

Scene Six

*The night of the same day. None of the room's original décor remains.
Everything is a mess. The curtains have been removed, replaced by
trousers. Along the walls there are garlands fashioned from shirts tied
together by their sleeves and interwoven with others made from petticoats
and bodices. Pieces of furniture have been made from pieces of what
was there previously, tied together with strips of cardigan, torn blankets
and bedspreads. The lights which hung from the ceiling are on the floor,
those on the floor hang from the ceiling. The walls are covered with
drawings and childish figures outlined with burnt cork: 'The Cat', 'The
Bad Man', 'The Hand', etc. There are also phrases: 'I am good',
'Christ the King', 'God is at my right hand', 'Long live me!' In short,
nothing is as it should be. A cyclone has passed through the room. The
only things that retain some semblance of having been arranged
deliberately are the paper flowers, huge paper flowers which are both
new and more numerous and which are everywhere over the floor.*

Eva *is standing in the middle of the chaos. She is having a bridal
gown fitted by the* **Barracuda** *who, with great care, arranges it on
her body.*

Barracuda (*pinning, making pleats*)   You see? Worth it,
wasn't it? Bit of patience, going through the old trunk? It's a
bit tight, of course, a bit rumpled here and there . . . but I
bet you never thought you'd get a second chance, eh? (*He
moves away, studies his work.*) . . . Assuming you had a first! (*He

adjusts a pleat.) There! A bit tight on the hips, maybe . . .
that's too many calories . . . or you getting on a bit, . . . or
letting yourself go . . . but it's not bad at all . . . (*He fixes
another pleat. He is the tailor who addresses the customer in a friendly
and suggestive manner.*) Pity it was pushed right down to the
bottom. I think I know why: a tram passing by, a hand
waving, a word not spoken, all the things we imagined . . .
so stick it in the bottom of the trunk! But what about the
bells, eh? The pretty little bells? And the laughing at the
entrance to the church? And the quick kiss on the cheek?
'Goodbye, Maria, we hope you live happy ever after!' 'Hope
everything goes well!' Doesn't all that matter? We shouldn't
be so hard on time . . . Things have a right to take revenge.
We can't expect them to adjust unless we give them a
helping hand.

*He moves away, approaches again, sees something wrong in the design,
rips one side of the dress.*

Perhaps rip the material to show the skin.

*He tears a piece of cretonne form the chair at his feet and uses it to
patch the torn dress. He smiles.*

The young brides! Oh, yes, I've seen them! I've watched
them from the park opposite the church, hidden in the
myrtle bushes . . . not that I'm a pervert, mind, or felt any
kind of jealousy . . . Why should I when I've got my paper
and my scissors?

He rips another part of the dress and patches it with a strip of cretonne.

See how they come through the tall grass, hardly touching
the ground, floating over the rye grass, trembling over the
damp fields . . . measured steps . . . all aglow . . . soft, white
undulations, weaving their way amongst the oak trees . . .
straight towards the sunlit steps   straight towards the
gloved hand. (*Whispering to her.*) And there, at that very
moment, watched by the drooling, hideous dwarfs
concealed behind the atrium walls deep in shadow, I've seen
them . . . I've seen them . . . (*He chokes, trembles.*) I've seen

them open the petals of their bodies . . . and offer . . .
imagine! . . . Offer . . . (*Shouting.*) offer . . . (*Calmer.*) their
virgin corollas to love's sweet consummation . . . ! (*A choked
cry.*) My God!

The **Barracuda** *controls himself and reverts to his joking tone. He
tears a sleeve, replaces it with another one made from a strip of paper.*

Others see it differently, of course. Take Fred . . . One day
we were there, in the bushes. He'd nicked a couple of tins of
oysters and there we was about to enjoy them . . .

He cuts the hem of the skirt with the scissors.

I ought to say that Fred has a way of chewing, a way of
moving the food around his mouth that's . . . noisy to say
the least . . . as if he's scared it'll go too fast to his guts and
he'll lose the pleasure of tasting every tiny bit. To be quite
honest, I can't say if it was his chewing, or the tension I was
feeling then, or the stone under my elbow . . . a bleedin'
stone had got there, see . . . a stone right under my elbow
. . . The thing is, I don't know if it was his chewing, or the
stone, or the tension I was feeling . . . To be quite honest, he
gets on my wick does Fred . . . I have to admit he drives me
barmy . . . I don't know if it was that or something else . . .
you know . . . him being disgusting, him being, no two ways
about it, completely revolting, or the stone, or the tension I
was feeling . . . The thing is I'm looking towards the church
and I say to him, 'Take a look', and he says to me, 'Those
bitches! Those bitches!' And I take a look at his ugly mug
and I see the juice from the oysters running from the
corners of his mouth . . . and his great red, bloodshot eyes . .
. and his noisy, disagreeable, disgusting, sickening way of
chewing . . . And the thing is, I feel something here inside
. . . a kind of uncontrollable tension . . . and I grab the other
tin of oysters . . . already opened but not yet eaten, see, and
I squash it, grind it, screw it, oysters and all, into his
revolting face. (*The preceding lines are shouted aloud. He calms
himself, becomes angelic.*) At that moment the bells of the
church rang out and I knew I'd done what I had to do . . .

I'd done my duty . . . Because people like Fred don't know, can't guess, have no conception of what a thing it is, what a wonderful thing to offer one's virginity! (*He emphasises the words, they are empty of real meaning.*) The . . . most . . . mag – ni – fi – cent . . . offer – ing . . . of . . . love! (*He laughs, amused by his own idea.*) Love is a broken bridge, with a broken tooth, with a broken crank. It flies within the world's four walls, cracking skulls. Love is a three-legged dog! A tramp with one hand and two bananas!

He has ripped away most of the skirt and is replacing it with pieces of curtain and strips of his own shirt. He looks at **Eva**, *concerned.*)

Anything wrong? Are you shivering?

Eva *trembles, just as the* **Barracuda** *often tembles.*

Are you cold? Are you hot? What is it? (*Pause. He waits.*) Do you want to take a stroll along the beach with the happy bridegroom? Collecting shells? Hand in hand, collecting . . . Discussing how many, what sex, what names, how many, what sex the kids will have that your golden future has in store? The arrangement of the furniture . . . the cretonne . . . the colours . . . 'No, it's better here', 'No, its better there' . . . the shapes . . . the cretonne . . . the bits of furniture . . . (*Speeding up.*) The position . . . the cretonne . . . the shapes . . . the number . . . the kids . . . the furniture . . . the shapes . . . the kids . . . Discussing love! Love with an 'l', an 'o', a 'v', an 'e', with everything, with passion, with no passion! The possibilities . . . of being, of achieving, of scarpering . . . of love . . . of solitude . . . of death . . . of getting there . . . of getting there . . . (*Shouting.*) Of getting there . . . of getting there . . . of gett – tt – ing th – e – re! (*He pants.*) Is that it? Is that the secret of the fridge? (*Of the bridal gown only the veil is left. The rest is a ragbag.*) Funny, isn't it? We are like two brothers.

He rips off the rest of his shirt. He covers his head with a paper rosette that looks like a crown. Long strips of paper hang down from it as far as his waist. He picks up a piece of wood and brandishes it like a spear.

Look! Ukulele, the Simba warrior!

He circles around **Eva**, *making grotesque movements and pulling funny faces.*

Uku! Azahamba! Humba! Tekeke! Takamba! Tumba! Last night I ate a little white nun . . . she tasted of soap! (*He laughs, looks at his hands.*) I'd chopped her into tiny bits, like the bits of meat you boil in soup. I spent the night seeing how many I could hold in my hand! (*He looks at her like an orang-utan watching its prey with curiosity. His face approaches her.*) Comment allez-vous, madame? Did you say something?

Eva (*with an effort*)   I . . .

Barracuda   Yes?

Eva   I

Barracuda   Yes?

Eva   I only . . .

Barracuda   You only . . . yes?

Eva   I only . . .

Barracuda   You only . . . yes? You said that once . . . You only . . .

Eva   I only . . .

Barracuda   Yes?

Eva *tries to speak but cannot. She makes an effort but in vain and then gives up. Pause.*)

Barracuda   You only wanted to love me, and me to love you. Right? (**Eva** *nods weakly.*) Yes, but it's far too late for that. Ukulele's guts are in his hands and he doesn't know what to do with them.

He places a large paper flower in **Eva**'s *bodice, so large it covers her face. He takes her arm in his.*

Shall we go?

Someone knocks on the door.

Yeah! Coming! (*He looks at* **Eva** *with compassionate concern, like a considerate fiancé.*) Ready then? (*Suddenly frightened.*) What are you doing? Crying? Laughing? Crying? Laughing? Stop crying! Stop laughing! Stop crying, I'm telling you! (*Louder, shouting.*) Stop laughing! Stop crying! If you don't stop crying, we can't go on! (*His expression suddenly changes, as is his wont. Sententious, empty, wordy.*)

The important thing's to have understood the game. To believe in each other. Mutual trust. To renounce yourself for someone else's sake, to the point where you and that someone else, where you . . . yourself . . . and that someone else . . . where you . . . Don't you fully agree?

Eva *nods weakly.*

Are we ready then?

Eva *is ready. Mendelssohn's 'Wedding March'. They begin to walk. 'Ukulele' walks stiffly, almost pathetic in his dignity, half-naked, covered only in rags; on his head the crown of paper with its hanging shreds.* **Eva** *is at his side, her arm in his, lost beneath the huge paper flower. The only real thing about her is the veil.*

Before we get there, you ought to know about the ins and outs of the river, the dangers you might encounter. There are some dangerous pits out there, and on certain nights when the moon's full and the river's full of broken furniture . . . people have been known to fall and break their neck . . .

They leave. In the room, complete disorder. Everything broken. There remains only the new kind of beauty: the dark, enormous, ragged paper flowers.

Medea in the Mirror

by

José Triana

This translation of *Medea in the Mirror* was first performed at the Brixton Shaw Theatre, London, on 27 June 1996, with the following cast:

Maria	Angela Wynter
Erundina	Sharon D. Clarke
Señorita Amparo	Faith Tingle
Julián	Jason James Pethers
Perico Piedra Fina	Dominic Letts
Chorus:	Lenny Algernon-Edwards
	Paul Jacuson James
	Jaqueline Mason
Flautist	Francesca Hanley

Directed by Yvonne Brewster
Designed by Ellen Cairns
Lighting by Dennis Charles
Movement by Jackie Guy and Greta Méndez
Sound by Stuart Saunders

Characters

Maria, *mulata*
Erundina, *an old black servant*
Señorita Amparo, *mestiza, very skinny*
Julián, *white, handsome*
Perico Piedra Fina, *white, fat, fifty*
Madam Pitonisa
Doctor Mandinga

Chorus:
Boy *selling newspapers and lottery tickets*
Barber, *white, long hair*
Antonio's Wife, *mulata, very fat*
Bongoman

The action takes place a few years back in the patio of a tenement block.

Act One: Midday and early evening
Act Two: Night and the early hours of the morning
Act Three: Dawn and morning

Act One

Scene One

Maria *alone. When the curtain rises she is centre stage. The distant sound of children singing.*

Maria   No, I can't be sure. I must control myself. But . . . why should this happen now, at the very moment I want to sit and be able to breathe? I have to be very careful. The others want me to pounce. I see it written in their faces. No need to try to work out its meaning. Can you ever imprison a cat? But faith and strength shall be my weapons. Julián loves me. Julián is the father of my children. Julián, Julián. My destiny is you.

Scene Two

Erundina *enters stage left.*

Maria   I shall discover what's going on.

Erundina (*whispering*)   Maria, Maria.

Maria   What do you want?

Erundina   I've been looking for you everywhere.

Maria (*fanning herself*)   I can't breathe inside there. Those rooms are getting on my nerves.

Erundina   You have to come inside.

Maria   What's all the rush?

Erundina   It's very important.

Maria   What do you mean?

Erundina   Come inside.

Maria   But I don't want to.

Erundina   I've brought the mirror.

Maria   The mirror?

Erundina   Right.

Maria   So what am I supposed to do with it?

Erundina   Look at yourself. (*Pause.*) You didn't sleep a wink last night.

Maria   Were you watching me?

Erundina   You haven't closed your eyes for nights on end.

Maria   Are you sure you aren't from the Salvation Army?

Erundina   Remember who you are, Maria. Besides, it will soon be Carnival.

Maria   I am getting old, Erundina.

Erundina   You are playing the corpse to see what kind of funeral you'll get.

Maria (*ironically*)   I have to find out what's going on.

Erundina (*mockingly*)   Then you'll need to consult the Spiritualist Centre.

Maria   Has Julián come back?

Erundina   Why do you ask? (*Pause.*) Have you seen him?

Maria   No.

Erundina   Well then . . .

Maria (*interrupting*)   Then I'll have to call Madam Pitonisa. I need advice.

Erundina   Do you think it's because of witchcraft that Julián has disappeared from your house? Do you think a pack of cards will tell you why?

Maria   Don't contradict me.

Erundina   I want to help you.

Maria   I haven't asked you to.

Erundina   I care for your children.

Maria (*surprised*)   For my children? (*Desperate.*) Where are they?

Erundina   In the backyard, with Carmelina's children.

Maria   I don't want to see them.

Erundina   Poor things! How are they to blame? When I left, they had finished their tea. They were playing with their dolls. That was when Salustiano arrived . . . at that very moment. He's nothing but skin and bone, you know. It seems he isn't getting on with his wife. At least, that's what he told me. He told me too he's very concerned about Julián's disappearance. That's all the people are talking about. Maria, listen to me. What's going to become of you? Could it be he's peddling drugs again? Remember what happened on Christmas Eve. The police might have picked him up.

Maria   Be quiet.

Erundina   But he's always done that sort of thing. What's so special now?

Maria   I said be quiet.

Erundina   If it bothers you, all right. (*As if she were talking to someone else.*) It's not as if I haven't told her . . . Maria, why are you so foolish? Why don't you use your common sense? . . . It's just like talking to a wall. She takes no notice. (*To* **Maria**.) You'll see what Juliancito's going to do to you. You'll see soon enough. (*Again as if she were talking to some unseen person.*) This woman is so stubborn. It's like an obsession. Something stuck inside her head, and she won't leave it as long as she lives. (*To* **Maria**.) They are saying that Perico Piedra Fina's up to something. That man's an agent of the Devil.

Maria   You always like to exaggerate. What do you mean?

Erundina   It's the truth. The absolute truth.

Maria (*laughing*)   The truth. Erundina seeks the truth. Erundina tries to deceive me with the truth. The truth you can buy on street corners, or in el chino Miguel's bar. The truth is the same whether it's a mango or an orange. (*In a different tone of voice.*) You are mad, Erundina. Completely mad.

Erundina   Face the truth, Maria. There's still enough time.

Maria   You've always liked your little joke.

Erundina   Think, think, think until you get beyond the boundary.

Maria   If only I could.

Erundina   If you hide yourself, if you hide yourself like a stupid girl, you'll never get there.

Maria   I always see what's there in front of me.

Erundina   Which is why you're always in the dark.

Maria   You think so?

Erundina   I do.

Maria (*playful*)   Then I am what I am.

Erundina   So short-sighted. Remember no one can avoid the truth.

Maria   It feels as if it's going to rain.

Erundina   I've had enough. You are driving me crazy. You stick in my throat.

Maria   Is that the way to speak to your mistress? You told me a lie, Erundina. I don't believe you went to a convent school. I shall have to take charge of my children's education.

Erundina   Take charge?

Maria   I think so, yes.

Erundina   But, Maria . . .

Maria   They shan't be exposed to all this nonsense. I'll see to it myself. (*Looking at her scornfully.*) Let's change the subject. I'll call Señorita Amparo. She will receive new instructions. (*She produces a whistle from her bosom, as well as a sprig of basil. She crosses herself.*)

Domestic affairs are such a problem. (*She blows the whistle.*)

Erundina (*as if she were talking to someone else*)   What is this woman trying to do? (*In a confidential tone of voice.*) It was me . . . this half-starved person you see here . . . who washed her nappies when she was still a baby. It was me . . . because her mother died in childbirth, and because my poor Evaristo had a heart of pure gold and was her father's friend . . . He said to me: 'Put her in her cradle, bring her here, and raise her up to be a good woman.' And there she was, so tiny, and there was me feeling so sorry for her . . . (*Change of tone.*) Has she gone crazy?

Scene Three

Señorita Amparo *enters. She is between thirty and thirty-five. She wears a dress with a flowered pattern. Her hair is pulled back into an enormous bun.*

Amparo (*to* **Maria**)   Good day to you. (*They embrace.*)

Erundina   I don't believe it. (*Looking at* **Señorita Amparo** *with distaste.*) It's just like hugging a plucked cockatoo!

Maria (*to* **Señorita Amparo**)   A good day to you.

Erundina   Have you ever seen such courtesy?

Amparo (*to* **Maria**, *cautiously*)   You wanted to see me?

Erundina (*speaking to an invisible person*)   I shall pretend. Maria must not think I am dying of envy.

Maria   We have important matters to discuss. Before we do, tell me what time you got here.

Amparo   A quarter past nine on the dot.

Maria   I call that lazy. That's just like having a good time. Aren't you satisfied with what I pay?

Amparo   Of course I am. What happened was that I had to go to the hospital . . . to take some oranges to the sister-in-law of one of my mother's god-daughters . . . And the main road . . .

Maria   Don't try to tell me a tall story!

Amparo (*scared*)   I'm not, señora. The main road . . .

Maria   I don't want excuses.

Amparo   The main road . . .

Erundina (*loudly*)   That main road is a real nightmare. The other day I went to get my medicine. The Caballero de París, you know, prescribed it for those dizzy spells of mine. In order to get it, I found myself at the end of an enormous queue in the Plaza de la Fraternidad, and after a while I got my cold sweats again and the people there looked after me until the Red Cross came . . .

Amparo (*to* **Erundina**, *scornfully*)   Interrupting us with all that nonsense! Must you be so common?

Erundina   Show some respect for these grey hairs. (*In a different tone.*) Your mother is quite crazy but people show respect for her.

Maria (*violently*)   Enough of that! (*Sweetening her expression.*) Señorita Amparo, I want you to feel at home amongst us. I'll see to it you get more sweet potato.

Amparo   That's good of you. That will be nice.

Maria   Even so, you have to learn to be more punctual. (*Short pause. Seriously.*) As from now, Erundina is excluded from my children's education.

Erundina   Maria, how can you play such a trick on me?

Maria   Those are my orders!

Erundina (*an outburst of fury*)   Sabotage! Sabotage!

Amparo   Orders have the force of reason.

Erundina   I didn't think her capable. I've sacrificed myself for her. But you know what they say: 'Raise ravens and they'll pluck your eyes out.'

Amparo (*phlegmatically*)   May I go?

Maria   Wait a moment. When are you starting the Physical Education classes? Wednesday, right? I shall be generous. I'll give you two pesos more.

Amparo   Oh, thank you, señora. Thank you. Oh, Holy Virgin of Regla, let your light shine on this woman. (*She falls on her knees.*) You can't imagine, señora Maria, the problems such an increase will solve. I'll do whatever you want whenever you want it.

Maria   Oh, please get up. It's not such a big thing really. Just a sisterly gesture. (*Looking at* **Erundina** *meaningfully.*) I am the one to benefit. It's good to know my children are in safe hands. (*Pause.*) Let's be frank with each other.

Erundina   Why don't you check if I'm right or not?

Maria (*to* **Erundina**)   Who said *you* could come to this funeral?

Erundina (*poking fun*)   Oh, aren't you the mournful one, Maria!

Maria   Let's be clear, señorita Amparo. (*Pause. Very quickly.*) It's a well-known fact, as experience has shown, that (*Becoming melodramatic.*) other people determine a woman's behaviour . . . (*Change of tone.*) Since I was this small (*Suggesting her size with the tip of her finger.*), old Erundina has always advised me. (*Change of tone.*) But lately you can't even talk to Erundina. Old age has simply magnified her faults.

Amparo   Señora, please, I beg you . . .

Maria   What?

Amparo   Don't be so flippant.

Erundina (*to* **Señorita Amparo**)   No, let her say what she wants to.

Maria   Where was I? Ah, yes. Old Erundina used to say: 'A woman is like a rose. No one dares to touch its petals. Don't talk about it. Admire it. Smell its perfume. A word can damage it for good.'

Amparo (*as if addressing another person*)   What's the point of all this rigmarole?

Maria   The fact is that someone has organised a tremendous show in order to destroy me.

Amparo   Destroy you?

Maria   That's what I said.

Erundina   You can't be serious.

Maria   By using the tactics of a hint here, a nudge-nudge there, they achieve a huge success. 'Maria's done this, Maria's done that.' You know what I mean?

Erundina   Are you suggesting I . . . ?

Maria   Did you hear me mention your name?

Erundina   You are driving me crazy.

Maria   Don't be so dramatic.

Erundina   But I . . .

Maria   Why are you getting so worked up? Just fifteen minutes ago you claimed that my childhood friend, Salustiano, who nowadays lives on the other side of the city, came to my room mysteriously frightened.

Erundina   It's the truth.

Maria   So, may I ask what was the source of those fears?

Erundina (*confused*)   I don't know. (*Firmly.*) You'd better ask her.

Maria   You are making it all up.

Erundina   Making it all up? (*Grabbing* **Señorita Amparo** *by the arm. Not knowing what to do, the* **Señorita** *coughs and scratches her nose.*) You tell her if Salustiano came. You tell her if he's playing with the children. You tell her if he wasn't speaking with Julián for a long time. Go ahead and tell her. Stop standing there looking like an idiot!

Amparo (*feeling trapped*)   Well, to tell you the truth . . . the fact of the matter is . . .

Erundina   Get it out, woman. Tell her what he said . . . Have you gone and lost your voice? Has the cat got your tongue?

Maria   Nothing but bad luck ahead!

Erundina   It looks as if Señorita Amparo is somewhat flummoxed.

Maria   Nothing but misfortune. What is it that the others know and dare not tell? What is it lies in store for me, O darkest of dark shadows? Cancer? Tuberculosis? (*Banishing a terrible vision.*) Leprosy? Has my body been touched by the Devil's sores? Oh, leprosy, leprosy!

Erundina (*to* **Maria**)   Put your trust in her. She is your salvation. She'll make of you what I once did. Here you have her, and I am now the guilty party. I am now the one to be despised. Such is the part you think I play. Erundina can't see straight. Erundina's mind is muddled. Erundina's in cloud cuckoo land!

Maria (*moving around, breathing heavily*)   Everything tells me I'm a piece of common gossip for the neighbourhood. (*Mocking herself.*) That I'm a rose about to fade away! . . . What can I do? . . . Maria Candela, what can I do? (*Pause. Change of tone.*) In the face of all this, I shan't give in. I shall be strong. I'll make a stand.

Erundina   Have faith, have faith! From this day on Señorita Amparo will be your faithful dog. Go ahead, Maria. Don't stop now. Señorita Amparo will care for your children, morning and afternoon. Señorita Amparo will be your pack-mule. Señorita Amparo is perfection!

Amparo (*confused*)   In that case . . .

Maria (*interrupting her*)   Let's look at my situation. Julián has disappeared from home at least a month.

Amparo (*feigning*)   Disappeared?

Erundina   Disappeared. As if you didn't know . . . Hypocrite!

Maria   Not that it's that important, depending on your point of view. From time to time Julián goes off on his little journeys.

Amparo   The other day I was passing cousin Berta's house, Candelaria's stepdaughter. I heard them saying something of the sort.

Maria (*expansively*)   Men, you know, have very private habits . . . But I understand them. Business, friends, drinking sessions, indiscretions . . . you know the sort of thing . . . Life can be so boring!

Amparo   Whoever saw a carry-on like this!

Erundina (*fanning herself with a handkerchief, wiping the perspiration from her face*)   I shall have to call Doctor Mandinga or Madam Pitonisa.

Amparo   In any case . . .

Erundina   Maria should not continue in this condition. She'll either end up looking like a beanpole or a patient at the Institution.

Amparo   I can assure you . . .

Erundina   It's a good thing that her mother, God rest her soul, can't see all this! Otherwise she'd have a heart attack.

Maria   When I stop to think of what I've been, of how I've sacrificed myself! . . . But the worst thing is that everyone is pushing me towards the void, towards my dead father, towards my brother who hanged himself.

Erundina (*crying out*)   I know what it is!

Amparo   My God, you scared me! Control yourself, woman!

Erundina   The evil eye!

Amparo   The evil eye?

Erundina   The evil eye!

Amparo   Don't make me laugh.

Erundina   Someone's put the evil eye on her.

Amparo (*splitting her sides with laughter*)   The evil eye!

Erundina   If it isn't that, she'll have to see a psychiatrist.

Maria   What's the matter with you, Erundina?

Erundina   Maria's going crazy. Maria isn't Maria.

Maria   What are you saying? (*Sarcastically.*) Maria needs no one. (*Solemn but simultaneously ridiculous.*) Maria wants something more important: to know what people really think. (*Pause. Approaching* **Señorita Amparo**.) Tell me! Tell me everything!

Amparo   What thing, señora?

Maria You know.

Amparo   I do?

Maria   You have to.

Amparo   Is it my duty?

Maria   Remember the money I pay you.

Amparo   I hope you don't think I sell myself.

Maria   Don't worry.

Amparo   You want me to be honest?

Maria   What else would I want you to be?

Amparo   I said to my mother this morning, you know: 'I don't want to get involved. Definitely not.'

Maria   I can see which way you are jumping, you vixen. Is getting involved all that's worrying you? Who puts the food in your mouth?

Amparo   Have I got to take sides?

Erundina (*to the* **Señorita**)   Don't pretend! (*Change of tone.*) Señorita Amparo, she cuts no ice with us. We know which side your bread is buttered.

Amparo   Señora, you are forcing me.

Erundina   Spill the beans!

Maria   I'm not forcing you. I'm asking you to help me out.

Amparo   I'd rather help you in the kitchen.

Maria   Who are you afraid of?

Amparo   Afraid of?

Erundina   Afraid of!

Amparo   Perico Piedra Fina's wife wouldn't want it spread around.

Maria   What are you talking about?

Erundina (*to* **Maria**)   You'll soon find out.

Maria (*to* **Erundina**)   Don't make me lose my temper! (*To* **Señorita Amparo**.) Answer me.

Amparo   It's a little complicated.

Maria   What has Perico Piedra Fina's wife got to do with all this?

Amparo   She is the mother.

Maria   Whose mother?

Amparo   The daughter's.

Maria   Which daughter?

Amparo   The mother's daughter.

Maria (*going crazy*)   'The mother, the daughter, the mother's daughter; the daughter, the mother, the daughter's mother.' What sort of cock and bull is this? I doubt the doctor could find a cure.

Amparo   All right . . . (*She looks around in all directions. The soft sound of maracas.*) It's too late to go back. Although I know you'll take revenge.

Maria (*laughing hysterically*)   Revenge? Revenge? Why use that awful word? Do you think that I'm the Vampire Woman?

Amparo   I know which card I'm going to play.

Maria   Then play it!

Amparo   I can see beyond it into the future.

Maria   Do you mean the ghosts of the dead appear to you at night?

Amparo   Do I have to tell you?

Maria   You have to.

Erundina   What an obstinate woman this is.

Amparo   All right, but don't come to me afterwards and tell me that I told you, or that I didn't tell you enough, or that I told you more than I should.

Maria   You tell me everything.

Erundina   Without even blinking.

Amparo   I'll tell you just as I was told. This morning . . . it must have been seven or half-past seven, I went to Dominga's house, the daughter of Carmelina's first husband . . . you know, the sergeant who fancied his chances with the girls and later became a stowaway . . . Well, Dominga came and told me everything . . . rely on her for the latest news.

Maria   What news was it she told you?

Amparo   That Perico Piedra Fina's wife was dead against it.

Maria   Against what?

Amparo   The marriage.

Maria   Whose marriage?

Amparo   Whose do you think? Her daughter, Esperancita.

Maria (*laughing*)   You mean that scarecrow's getting married at last?

Amparo   Her father, old Perico . . . his father was a colonel in the times of Don Tomás . . . is over the moon with the wedding . . . And later this evening, Julián . . .

Maria (*almost whispering*)   Julián.

Amparo (*smiling cruelly*)   Yes, Julián . . . Julián Gutiérrez, later this evening, is going to marry Esperancita, the daughter of Perico Piedra Fina.

Maria   Julián intends to marry that crook's daughter?

Erundina (*shouting*)   So!

Amparo (*coming downstage*)   I didn't know if I should come to teach your children. But then I thought you might have agreed to it . . . There are plenty of examples . . .

Maria (*upstage*)   Julián getting married? (*Laughs hysterically.*) Julián getting married? It must be a joke. Getting married to Esperancita.

Erundina   She's nothing but a bag of bones, a scarecrow. A man would have to be completely shameless.

Maria   It's the most amazing thing this year! (*Pause.*) Señorita Amparo, am I above or below ground? (*Pause.*) Go on!

Amparo   My father's eighty years of age, but even so he threw me out.

Maria   Are you quite sure of your facts?

Erundina   Esperancita's got herself out of a spot. She'd have spent the rest of her life in meditation.

Maria   (*to* **Erundina**)   Stop interrupting!

Erundina   Leave me alone. Julián's a good-for-nothing.

Maria (*to* **Erundina**)   I'll put a gag in your mouth! (*To* **Señorita Amparo**.) Get on with it!

Amparo (*downstage*)   My mother was shouting: 'Stop being a fool. It's no good crying. You have to accept things as they are. If you are afraid, put your fear in the rubbish-bin.'

Maria   Stop beating about the bush, woman!

Erundina (*to the* **Señorita**)   No need to be scared!

Maria   Finish the story.

Amparo   I don't know if I've acted properly.

Maria   Don't be such a timid creature.

Amparo   I might regret it afterwards.

Maria   We haven't got all day.

Erundina   We haven't got all week either.

Maria   Do we have to wait for eternity?

Amparo   They were shouting in the street. (*Aside.*) I know this isn't wise.

Maria   What were they shouting? Who was shouting?

Erundina   How long were they shouting, woman?

Amparo   I can't, I can't.

Maria   You must, you must.

Erundina   The end, the end.

The three women are linked to each other and begin to move rhythmically. The scene acquires a rhythmic sound.

Amparo (*mechanically*)   In the street, the square, the park, the bar, the cinema, the café, the bus . . . knock-kneed Chencha, Rosa la China, Cachita Burundanga, Antonio's wife, Pedro's wife, Chucho's wife, Jacinto's wife, José's wife, told me, tell me, keep telling me, that you are, you were, you will be, always, now, never, you are, you were, you will be, at the corner of this nameless building waiting for the call of blood.

The women separate. Pause. **Maria** *moves as if in a dream.*

Erundina (*softly*)   Maria, Maria.

Amparo (*very softly*)   Maria.

Erundina (*softly*)   Maria.

Amparo (*very softly*)   Maria.

Maria (*overcome*)   Leave me alone. I need to get some air. I'm choking in this oven.

The stage grows steadily darker. **Señorita Amparo** *sinks slowly to her knees. Only* **Maria** *is illuminated.*

Maria (*as if addressing someone else*)   Maria, what have you done? You had to know.

Erundina   What could you know that you didn't know before?

Maria (*wearily*)   What I must do with the future.

Erundina   Maria will handle the future as if it were a plateful of tamales.

Maria   Maria is in the dark. Maria will always struggle. Maria wants to know, to know. (*Pause.*) Oh, it's so, so dark! Julián, my beautiful Julián! (*Pause.*) Can we ever find any goodness in this world of ours? (*Pause.*) I am walking in darkness. My children. Show me the way ahead. Which way should I go? Show me the way!

Erundina *falls to her knees, opposite* **Señorita Amparo**.

Scene Four

The light returns to normal revealing **Maria**, **Erundina**, **Señorita Amparo** *and the* **Boy** *who sells newspapers and lottery tickets.* **Maria** *stands motionless.*

Boy (*calling out*)   Eighty-three, eighty-four. Who wants these numbers?

Scene Five

*The **Barber** enters stage right. He wears a uniform and carries a pair of scissors.*

Barber (*moving the scissors noisily, talking to someone*)   I tell you, sir. A tragedy. What you would call a real tragedy.

Boy   Tragedy. Tragedy. Six-two-eight-three, a marriage ends in tragedy. Six-two-eight-four, a marriage ends in blood. Pay attention!

Barber   Pay proper attention. I assure you I know this tenement from top to bottom. Don't make such a noise. Remember Perico Piedra Fina's orders. (*Grandiloquently.*) The loathsome owner of this place. If he hears you shouting, he'll make you pay a peso fine. No more, no less. We're all accustomed to it. He never leaves us alone. He's a kind of inquisitor. In colonial times, when they treated men like animals, the situation was no worse . . . But you are as ignorant as her . . . Tell Maria that Perico . . .

Scene Six

*Enter **Antonio's Wife**, a colourful mulata, who is carrying an enormous straw basket and containers full of vegetables and fruit.*

Wife   Perico, woman. Perico Piedra Fina . Do you mean some kind of abuse? Do you mean Julián?

Barber   Julián has always been king of the street corner, the billiard hall, of Estebita's bar. Ask anyone.

Wife   Anyone can tell you that. And – do you know? – he's all show. I promise you, woman, I know what the situation is. Julián is one of those who begins to straight away flatter you and draw you castles in the air. And if a girl is taken in, she's on the slippery slope and soon sent packing! He's all deception.

Barber   Deception or injustice is all that Perico Piedra Fina knows. They say he gave an order once and now it carries an official seal . . . Now in this case there's no one can accuse Maria . . . not in the entire world.

Boy   World news. World news. Extra. Stop press. Extra. All the latest in our country.

Wife   In our country it doesn't do to be dark-skinned, no matter where you go.

Barber   No matter where or whether she wants, she'll have to leave. It's not a question of 'Pay in a fortnight or else you're in the street.' This is a very different matter. Here is a woman alone with two small children. She can't put up a fight. Besides, who cares about the bitterness she has to swallow? No one.

Wife   No one can imagine it. How can anyone put up with such humiliation? Antonio was the first to tell me in the tobacconist's: 'Julián and Perico . . .' (*Sound of a motorcar horn.*) I suddenly felt so cold.

Barber   Cold in the middle of the afternoon, and in a summer as hot as this. Maria's the one who'll be feeling cold, believe me.

Boy (*approaching* **Maria**)   Believe me, señora. Try your luck here. It's your lucky day. The big prize. The big prize. Roll up! Six-two-eight-three, a marriage ends in tragedy! Extra. Roll up! Eighty-four, blood! Six-two-eight-four, a marriage ends in blood!

Wife   Blood, yes, blood! That's what he deserves. Julián will not be forgiven by God.

Barber   God? Do you have proof?

Wife (*shouting*)   Proof? You have it there. Look!

Barber   Look! The fiesta.

Wife   The fiesta. The bride and bridegroom have arrived. A fiesta that is an insult. Do you want me to be quiet?

Never. I shall shout it aloud. Let Perico Piedra Fina come. (*Pause.*) Julián, I want to see you in a pool of blood. (*Pause.*) An example to all others.

Scene Seven

Bongoman *enters stage left. He has a red cloth around his neck. He beats his drum softly.*

Bongoman (*laughing*)   An example. Such a naïve idea. Julián's got plenty of guts. He gets his own way, no matter what you say to him. Consider this fact. Since Julián has been with Maria, he hasn't looked at anyone else. For men like him, each minute is the last minute.

Boy   Last minute. Extra.

Wife   Extramarital? Do you think Maria could put up with such a situation?

Bongoman   Situation. Situation. All hot air in the face of reality.

Barber   Reality. Exactly. What liberties are taken by Julián.

Wife (*in a gossiping tone*)   Julián has a ring for Esperancita. It's worth . . .

Boy   A hundred thousand pesos.

Barber   A hundred thousand pesos.

Boy   Buy this number, favoured by good fortune. Six-two-seven-four, a marriage that ends in blood. 'World News', 'The Nation', 'World News'.

Bongoman   The world is a circle of blood.

Wife   Blood, blood, blood, always blood. Death.

Bongoman   Death, no. Death is like the ghost of the evil eye.

Barber   The evil eye?

Bongoman   Yes.

Boy   The evil eye.

Barber   The evil eye.

Bongoman   The evil eye.

Wife   Ah, now I know. Maria has the evil eye.

Bongoman   Maria has the evil eye.

Barber   Maria has the evil eye.

Wife   Maria has the evil eye.

Lights down slowly. The music of the drum. The **Chorus** *sings.*

Chorus
    Maria has the evil eye.
    The evil eye, the evil eye.
    Maria has the evil eye. Maria is cursed.
    Maria has the evil eye.
    The evil eye, the evil eye.
    Maria has the evil eye.
    Maria is cursed.

Scene Eight

Maria (*shouting*)   It isn't true. It isn't true. You are deceiving me. Leave me alone. Julián loves me. Julián is my husband. (*Pause.*) But why do they dare to say it? If they go on saying it, I am lost. Are they with me or against me? (*Pause.*) Or is it true a curse hangs over me? Erundina. Where is the mirror?

Erundina (*waking from a dream*)   The mirror?

Scene Nine

Maria   Yes, the mirror. (**Erundina** *tries to get up.*) Wait.
(*As if she were seeing* **Julián** *in the audience.*) Julián. Is that you?
I feel such joy! I was talking about you a moment ago. I
spend my life speaking your name. Erundina is always
taking me to task. She's old, she doesn't understand. I say to
her: 'Julián loves me. Julián is my husband. Julián is the
father of my children. Julián is my destiny.' (*Smiling.*) She
doesn't remember what love is. (*As if she were going to embrace
him.*) What does it matter what I am and what I was? What
do I care what freedom is if your arms are mine? (*Reacting as
if he rejects her.*) What's the matter? Do you have a headache?
Have you been playing poker? Did you lose much money?
(*Trying to embrace him again.*) Don't get downhearted. We've
gone through far worse times. Remember when my brother
was hanged on account of Perico Piedra Fina? . . . I swore
revenge. The jury believed he was innocent. They even
tried to involve you . . . How could evil escape like that?
They condemned him . . .

Scene Ten

Julián *appears behind* **Maria**. *He wears a white cotton shirt.*
Maria *turns to him. They begin to dance to the sound of the drum.*

Maria   Let's forget unpleasant things. Life is wonderful.
These days of separation have helped me greatly. I have
learned to understand that only you give any meaning to my
life. I shall try to be more understanding. Would you like a
drink of pineapple, or a slice of melón I've cut specially for
you? Would you like to see the menu for today? A nice bean
soup with just a touch of pepper. White rice, very fine, the
kind you like. Roast meat with lots of onion. Very special. I
got the recipe from Serafina, Evangelina's cousin, the one
who ran away with Candelaria's nephew . . . Oh, yes, and
aubergines fried in batter – if the angels were to see them,
they'd all fly down to earth! For dessert, a tasty apple-tart to

make you and the children suck your fingers afterwards.
Would you like me to prepare a bath for you? I'll put some
eau-de-Cologne in the water. Or maybe you prefer a
shower? Have you changed your vest and pants? At midday
yesterday I was darning your socks and sewing buttons on
your shirts . . . (*They stop dancing.*)

Julián   I came to look for you.

Maria   Wait a minute. Let me hold you. (*She embraces him.*)
I shouldn't say 'I love you' so often. You take advantage of
my feelings. I've spent some terrible nights alone. Where
were you all that time? The children never stopped asking
for their father. (**Julián** *pushes her away.*) What's wrong?
Don't you like me any more?

Julián   Don't be silly. They are waiting for us.

Maria   Who?

Julián   You'll find out soon.

Maria   Where are we going, Julián?

Julián   My little secret.

Maria   Tell me.

Julián   Don't you trust me? (*Taking her by the arm.*)

Maria (*disturbed*)   Who's waiting for us? Where are we
going?

Julián   How foolish you are. You always make mountains
out of molehills. (*Laughing.*) We are going to paradise.

Maria *cannot move. She does not know what to do or say. We begin
to hear the voices of the* **Chorus**, **Erundina** *and* **Señorita
Amparo**, *who are looking for the mirror. When* **Maria** *hears the
word 'mirror', she repeats it mechanically. The* **Chorus** *achieves an
ever-greater intensity.* **Maria**, *in a kind of swoon, searches for the
mirror in the air.*

Act Two

Scene One

Night. **Erundina** *stands in the doorway of* **Maria**'s *room. She seems overwhelmed. She looks in all directions and comes downstage.*

Erundina   Where can she be at such an hour? Could she have gone to see Madam Pitonisa or Doctor Mandinga? Perish the thought. (*Looking to the right.*) Oh, Maria, Maria. You must have got a screw loose. What other explanation is there? You told me to go looking for Julián. I didn't want to get involved, so I refused. But then you made such a fuss that I agreed. I went to look . . . a black woman looking for the Devil. But the Devil wasn't at home. (*Change of tone.*) When I got back, it was Maria who had disappeared. I hope she hasn't made a pact with him! (*Pause.*) You make me so nervous. I don't understand you, not one little bit. (*Transition.*) But why bother trying to understand her? When did I ever understand what was going through that head of hers?

Scene Two

Voice   What? But I've told you already. You'll see for yourself.

Erundina   I hear voices. Ave Maria, what a fuss there's going to be.

Voice   Erundina, Erundina.

Erundina   Who's there? (*Loudly.*) Who's calling me?

Voice   It's me, woman.

Erundina   Ah, you! Let me see you. (*Passing her hand across her stomach.*) Just tell me what you fancy doing.

Enter **Señorita Amparo**.

Amparo (*outraged*)   Don't be so disgusting. Do you think I'm the sort of person who spends her life bringing children into the world? I would never do that sort of thing. You know the sort of person I am.

Erundina   Woman, I was only joking.

Amparo   Have you heard the latest?

Erundina   Latest what?

Amparo (*singing*)   Latest surprise, of course.

Erundina   Surprise?

Amparo   Can't you guess?

Erundina   Some piece of gossip, I suppose!

Amparo (*upset*)   What do you mean?

Erundina   Exactly what I say.

Amparo   Explain yourself.

Erundina   What am I supposed to explain?

Amparo   What you've just said.

Erundina   Is it something from the other world?

Amparo   No need to insult me.

Erundina   I didn't mean to.

Amparo   Don't play the innocent.

Erundina   Could it have been that Perico Piedra Fina's wife was wearing the blue taffeta dress her grandmother gave her for the wedding?

Amparo   You think that I don't know what you are up to.

Erundina   So, what is that?

Amparo   You are trying to make me look a fool.

Erundina   Don't be silly, woman. No need to be so touchy. (*Change of tone.*) It couldn't have been that Esperancita had an abscess on her funny bone?

Amparo (*amused*)   That's an old one. Remember all the fuss? They almost had her on the operating table.

Erundina (*weary, sighs*)   I give up. I don't know.

Amparo   Why not have a guess?

Erundina   You want me to guess?

Amparo   Why not? That's how you discover the meaning of life.

Erundina   That's what I'm always doing. (*To herself.*) I was born to imagine. Let's see then . . . (*Change of tone.*) They are going to New York for the honeymoon?

The beating of a drum begins.

Amparo (*amused*)   Cold as ice. Try again.

Erundina   Perico Piedra Fina's hit the jackpot?

Amparo   I can't hear you.

Erundina (*almost shouting*)   Perico Piedra Fina's won the lottery?

Amparo   Those drums are making such a noise!

Erundina   Are you going to tell me?

Amparo   I can't hear you.

Erundina   They sent Perico's wife a bottle of wine from the Home Office.

Amparo   You'd better be careful. You might get arrested for saying that.

Erundina   I couldn't care less.

Amparo   It's something to do with Maria.

Erundina   Maria?

Amparo   A juicy bit of news.

Erundina   Tell me quickly.

Amparo (*with emphasis*)   Perico Piedra Fina . . .

Erundina   What about him?

Amparo (*suddenly*)   He came to see Maria.

Erundina   When?

Amparo   A short while ago. (*Arranging her hair.*)

Erundina   Are you quite sure?

Amparo   Cross my heart.

Erundina   They spoke together? (*Change of tone.*) Who told you?

Amparo (*fluttering her hands*)   A little bird.

Erundina   Spit it out. How can you say that *I* get on *your* nerves?

Amparo   I'm getting my own back.

Erundina (*beside herself*)   This is no time to be playing games.

Amparo (*unmoved, looking to the heavens*)   You have to guess.

Erundina   I hate this sort of carry-on.

Amparo   See if you can't get close.

Erundina   Why not tell me?

Amparo   You don't know?

Erundina   How can I know if no one tells me anything?

Amparo   Dominga.

Erundina (*laughing*)   You mean the one who sells 'churros' in the marketplace. The one that always . . .

Amparo   No, woman. Not her. Carmelina's daughter . . .

Erundina (*bursting in*)   She's better than the 'Official News Bulletin'.

Amparo   She saw them.

Erundina   Talking here?

Amparo   Of course not.

Erundina   Where, then?

Amparo (*amused, singing*)   Where, where . . . ?

Erundina (*loudly*)   Yes, where?

Amparo   On the jetty.

Erundina   Praise be to God!

Amparo   And Julianito was with them.

Erundina (*to herself*)   On the jetty. (*Change of tone.*) Maria dared do that?

Amparo   You can confirm it. (*The music of the drums has stopped. She laughs as she speaks.*) Do you know what she did? She gave old Perico a present – a bottle of wine she made herself. (*Pause.*) I saw her weeping a short time ago, on the corner by the billiard hall. (*Exaggerating.*) She seemed completely desperate. I felt for her. I wanted to console her, but I stopped myself . . . She looked so helpless . . . (*Exaggerated gesture.*) . . . like something out of control. (*Imitating her.*) She was weeping and saying over and over 'The mirror, the mirror.'

Erundina (*to herself*)   How could she, how could she, knowing what she knows? . . . where has she got to at such an hour? . . . Have they thrown her into the sea? Has she been eaten by the sharks? (*Shouting.*) Oh, sea, oh, sea, oh, sharks, oh, sharks, let me have her back! Where shall I look? Shall I go to the police station?

Amparo   To tell them what?

Erundina (*waving her arms*)   To tell them to investigate.

Amparo   To investigate what?

Erundina   I don't know. Something.

Amparo   Don't get excited.

Erundina   Do you expect me to twiddle my thumbs?

Amparo   I'm sorry.

Erundina   Oh, Maria. What will become of your children? (*Desperate, pacing around.*) What will become of them? What will become of me? Oh, Maria! What is your fate? (*Shouting.*) Where is the mirror?

Amparo (*alarmed*)   The mirror?

Erundina   Where is it? Where is it?

Amparo   Don't start to consult visions.

Erundina   It's the last straw. (*Going out, crying out, weeping.*) Let them get me a straitjacket!

Scene Three

The characters of the **Chorus** *appear, each in his or her doorway as in Act One.*

Wife (*singing*)   Perico Piedra Fina.

Barber (*singing*)   Perico Piedra Fina.

Bongoman (*singing*)   Perico Piedra Fina.

Boy (*singing*)   Perico Piedra Fina.

Chorus (*ending the song*)   Perico Piedra Fina.

Scene Four

Perico Piedra Fina *enters stage left. He is a greasy, slimy character with a high-pitched, fluting voice. He is fifty or so years of* *age. He is wearing a linen suit, a brilliantly coloured tie and a straw hat. He carries a walking stick.*

Perico   The one who runs the entire show. (*He twirls the stick and thumps it on the ground.*) Perico Piedra Fina.

Scene Five

Julián *enters. He is a young man, very handsome, tall, slim, in his twenties. He is wearing white trousers, a loose-fitting shirt and two-toned shoes. He has a showy chain around his neck and rings on his fingers.*

Julián (*indicating* **Perico**)   Here he is.

Perico (*bowing slightly, indicating* **Julián**)   Julián Gutiérrez, my daughter's husband. Take a look at him.

Julián (*taking a sweeping bow*)   At your service.

Chorus (*singing quietly*)
   He's going to die, he's going to die.
   Throw plenty of earth
   Where he lies.

Perico   Why sing those melancholy songs? Today is a day of rejoicing. Didn't you know. My daughter's just got married. My only daughter, Esperancita. Why such a long faces? I'm not the Bogeyman. You've made a mistake. (*To* **Julián**.) Do I look as if I'm mourning someone's death?

Julián (*smiling*)   Pay no attention. It's a joke.

Perico   Ah, yes, a joke.

Julián   They are amusing themselves.

Perico   Can't they see I'm dying of laughter?

Chorus (*whispering*)
   He's going to die, he's going to die.
   Throw plenty of earth
   Where he lies.

Perico   Have they finished? (*Looking at the* **Chorus**.) All right. We are here to celebrate a notable event.

Wife and **Boy**   A notable event?

Barber and **Bongoman**   A notable event?

Julián   Why so surprised?

Perico   Another joke?

Julián   You didn't know?

Wife and **Boy**   What should we know?

Barber and **Bongoman**   What should we know?

Perico   They couldn't have known, quite obviously.

Wife   It's a mystery.

Barber   A mystery.

Bongoman   It's a mystery.

Boy   A mystery.

Julián   No, there is no mystery.

Wife   Then what can it be?

Barber   What can it be?

Bongoman   What can it be?

Boy   What can it be?

Perico (*laughing*)   Be, be, be.

Wife and **Boy**   Be who, be what?

Barber and **Bongoman**   Be what, be who?

Perico (*amused*)   Stop this fooling about. I'm a practical person. Bread for me is bread, and wine wine.

Julián (*twisting one of his rings*)   Exactly.

Perico (*To* **Julián**)   How else could I have lived so long? Life is so hard.

Julián   That's why your money is hard-earned, Perico.

Perico (*putting his hand to his throat*)   This wine is burning my throat. (*Pause.*) If you want to know what's happened . . . (*Pause.*) Maria . . .

Wife   Maria . . .

Barber   Maria . . .

Bongoman   Maria . . .

Boy   Maria . . .

Perico   To tell you the truth, Maria . . .

Wife and **Boy**   What's happened to Maria?

Barber and **Bongoman**   What's happened to Maria?

Perico   For goodness sake, be patient. Nothing's happened to her. It's just that she's gone missing. Let's get it straight. She's gone on a little outing.

Wife   Outing.

Barber   Outing.

Bongoman   Outing.

Boy   Outing.

Perico   And why not? She has every right. All of us here know Maria.

Wife and **Boy**   All of us know her.

Barber and **Bongoman**   All of us know her.

Perico (*moving slowly*)   Let her enjoy her freedom. (*Sarcastically.*) Let her have her freedom.

Chorus (*moving arms and bodies in unison*)   Let her enjoy her freedom. Let her have her freedom.

Perico   Then why create such a fuss? She's got what she wants. Isn't that right, Julián?

Julián   No one can deny it.

Perico   Does anyone think I'm joking? You know I always tell the truth.

Wife and **Boy**   He always tells the truth.

Barber and **Bongoman**   He always tells the truth.

Perico   In that case, my friends . . . (*To* **Julián**.) Tell them up there to send down some rum . . . And don't forget the wine.

Julián *goes out.*

Scene Six

Perico   Let's have a real party! (*Pause. Contented.*) Have you seen Julián? Have you really seen him?

Wife   We've seen him.

Barber   We've seen him.

Bongoman   We've seen him.

Boy   We've seen him.

Perico   That makes me happy. The boy's not a fool. That's why I chose him. (*Thumping his chest.*) He's like me. I've seen it in his eyes. I know I'm right. (*Pause. Amazed.*) How can I be so sure? Because I'm Perico Piedra Fina. (*Laughing.*) I can see you've forgotten what that means. We are people who forget things easily. (*Pause. Change of tone. Fleeing from a strange vision.*) Oh, no, no. He isn't the sort to betray me or steal my money or do a disappearing act, leaving my daughter in the lurch. (*Change of tone.*) In any case, he'd never mange it. I'll play him along, keep him guessing. There's nothing quite so powerful as keeping alive someone's hopes of better things ahead. Just consider me as one example. Why, many years ago, Perico Piedra Fina, the very person standing here, sold doughnuts from a stall in the

Street of San Lázaro. (*Laughs.*) The years do not pass by in vain. (*Looking upwards.*) Don't you agree? It's almost like a fairy tale. (*Pause.*) I've sweated blood and tears. The friends I used to have now look on me with envy. 'There goes Perico,' they say, 'the one who sold his soul to the Devil.' So tell me: What's a soul, and who is the Devil? (*Pause.*) My friends now slap me on the back and can't stop saying: 'Aren't you the lucky one, Perico?' (*Laughing.*) Tell me what and who luck is. (*Pause. Darkly.*) The only thing I know for sure is that behind most things there is a nightmare.

Wife   A nightmare.

Barber   A nightmare.

Bongoman   A nightmare.

Boy   A nightmare.

Perico   What's happening here? (*Hitting the ground with his stick.*) Let's have some music, dancing! Begin the celebrations! I need a drink. (*Calling.*) Bring me a drink.

Wife   Bring me a drink.

Barber   Bring me a drink.

Bongoman   Bring me a drink.

Boy   Bring me a drink.

Scene Seven

Julián (*entering, happy, calling out*)   The drinks have arrived. (*He carries a tray with bottles and glasses.*) May there be rum until the Day of Judgment!

Perico   Thank God you've come back. (*Looking at the* **Chorus**.) These people are giving me a hard time. (*Pause. He takes the bottle quickly, sniffs at it. Pause. Change of tone.*) What were the servants doing? Why did you have to bring it yourself?

Julián   We live in a democracy. (*He begins to sing, an out-of-tune baritone.*)

Perico   You have to keep your distance.

Julián   It doesn't matter.

Perico   You've got to learn.

Julián   Don't worry about it. (*Singing.*) Life is short and the future an illusion.

Perico   Has anyone else come?

Julián   The people keep on asking for you.

Perico   Has Manengue arrived? Did he bring the mortgage documents?

Julián   You mean the senator's nephew? Yes, he did.

Perico   Has he signed them?

Julián (*producing some papers from his jacket pocket*)   See for yourself.

Perico (*checking the signatures*)   You have to be careful.

Julián   No one fools me.

Perico   I'm glad to hear it.

Julián (*change of tone*)   How can a man like that become the Minister of Education?

Perico   Keep calm. You close your mouth, you don't get flies in it. You'll get your opportunity. The man who has a godfather will get baptised.

Julián   It makes me boil to see things like that happen.

Perico   Leave things to me. (*He produces a wad of notes.*) Look, Julián. Look at this money. (*Pause. Grandiloquently.*) My kingdom is infinite.

Pause.

Julián   The brother of Juanito Cien Botellas arrived in an enormous car.

Perico   Perfect.

Julián   Important people. People of substance. I said to myself: 'Julián, this is Julián, who just a month ago was eating dust.' And I looked at myself in the mirror. We are in paradise. Life is a river of surprises. I am another Julián!

Perico   The only one to be trusted with my business affairs. (*Pause.*) And how is Esperancita?

Julián   Extremely nervous . . . Just now she started to cry and made a great show of herself. I calmed her down by telling her we'd go upstairs quite soon.

Perico   No need to worry. (*He sits down.*)

Julián   I feel sorry for her. There are so many guests.

Perico   Pay no attention. All women are the same. Give me some rum. Her mother used to cry for days on end, until she got accustomed to it. What else could she do? (*Looking at the bottle of wine.*) The wine looks good, Julián. Maria was really quite pleasant. I didn't expect her to be like that. Not when they say she's like a wild animal. She was so meek and mild . . . (*Laughing, sarcastic.*) Imagine her giving me this wine. This beautiful bottle! What brand is it? I can't read the label. I seem to have left my glasses somewhere. Probably in the sacristy. My wife's to blame with all her fussing. (*Change of tone. To* **Julián**.) To be quite frank, we've made her look a real fool, Julián. But what was I supposed to do? Just sit here and admire the view? (*He takes a drink.*) Perico Piedra Fina knows what makes the world go round. Maria, poor Maria, she had no time to be prepared. Perico Piedra Fina's far too smart. Of course, she loves you too much, Julián. Because of that, she could have jumped on me like a lioness.

Julián   Don't exaggerate. Maria will have to get used to it. The only thing that bothers me is my children.

Perico   Your children?

Julián Exactly.

Perico (*to the audience*)   And what about Esperancita?

Julián I'm concerned about them.

Perico (*getting up, approaching* **Julián**)   Put aside such thoughts. Maria will be a woman alone. I'll find some way of getting them from her. Perico Piedra Fina is an expert at pulling off such things.

Julián You don't need to tell me.

Perico So who's been drinking this wine?

Julián Wine?

Perico Look. Someone's taken a swig of it.

Julián Oh, Esperancita was trying it. She had a mouthful.

Perico You must be joking. It looks as if she took a fancy to it. Try it yourself. Excellent quality.

The characters of the **Chorus** *observe him. They are content.*

Julián (*jokingly*)   I need to stay sober . . . you know, for later on.

Perico The wine will get you more excited, man. It makes women look even better. I want to see my house full of grandchildren . . . lots of grandchildren.

Julián That must be why Esperancita was so insistent: 'Oh, don't go, I feel so cold. Oh, don't leave me.' A good thing I got her to rest for a while.

Perico (*pulls out a handkerchief, wipes his forehead*)   It's so damned hot. The night is like lead. (*Pause. To the* **Chorus**.) Why don't you enjoy yourselves? Let's have music. Let's beat the hell out of those drums. You up there. Set the place on fire. A night like this has to go on for ever. (*Cackles with laughter.*) Isn't that right, Maria? (*Shouting*) I am the master. I am the king.

Julián   It looks like the wine has gone to your head already.

Perico   Don't be a fool. Let's have music. Let's enjoy ourselves and all the rest can go to hell. (*He grabs* **Julián** *by the collar*.) More wine! More wine! Do you remember what I told Maria? Do you remember?

Julián   How can I forget?

Perico   That's good. (*Change of tone, as if he were speaking to* **Maria**.) Listen, Maria. Get out of here. Pack your things tonight and get out in the morning . . . with your things on your back if need be. If you don't do what I say, I'll send the police to pick you up. Remember your father and your brother, both of them dead. They didn't take my advice, you know. So you had better do it. (*Pause*.) What do you think? Did I get the better of her or not?

Julián (*pulling at* **Perico**)   Let's go.

Perico   Get your hands off me. No one tells me what to do. I'm Perico Piedra Fina and I do whatever I want.

A terrible cry is heard.

Julián   What's happened?

They leave quickly.

Scene Eight

Perico Piedra Fina *and the* **Chorus** *onstage.*

Perico   I couldn't care less. Let the great flood come and drown the world. (*Pause. The stage grows dark.*) What's all this nonsense? (*Banging his stick on the ground.*) What's this noise? Could it be the smell of trouble brewing? You know what I mean, Maria, just as well as I do. You grew up here. I used to see you almost every day. (*Twirling his stick.*) You see? I always have the luck. (*Laughs.*) Maria, beautiful Maria. (*He throws the bottle to one side.*) You are too fond of fairytales. Oh,

I don't blame you. I know about these things myself. But I always come back to earth. And I know exactly what my plans are. You'd best take care . . . everyone's afraid of me and so they play the game . . . But you . . . I gave you the room and you rented it out to Manengue and Manengue sold it to me . . . a real tangle, don't you think? I have the papers here. I got them from Julián just now. Maria, beautiful Maria. You are the queen of the witches, Snow White's wicked stepmother. I know that I am headed for death . . . I hear its footsteps . . . this damned wine . . . Where are you, Julián? (*He stumbles, starts to cough.*) I'm making a fool of myself. My father, a retired colonel, died of starvation. (*Sings.*) Aye, aye, aye. (*Change of tone.*) I feel so giddy, I feel so sick . . . I am a free Cuban . . . (*Almost singing.*) . . . who, when he sings, is dying . . . (*He laughs.*) in the night . . . a man who once sold fritters in the salon of Pasos Perdidos . . . (*He falls to the ground, centre stage, near* **Maria***'s door.*)

Wife (*to the* **Boy**)   Give me some more.

Barber (*amused, to the* **Wife**)   Don't be a glutton.

Wife (*to the* **Boy**)   Is this rum yours?

Boy   Cheeky woman. What if your husband saw you?

Wife   Give me the bottle.

Bongoman   Life has to be enjoyed, to the last drop.

Erundina (*offstage, calling out*)   Maria, the mirror.

Perico   A mirror of death. Don't mention the mirror. Don't look at me like that. You've poisoned the wine. You've poisoned the night. You've poisoned the hour.

Barber (*laughing, to the* **Wife**)   You'll drink yourself to death, you know.

Wife   That's my affair.

Barber (*amused*)   You see. Antonio's coming.

Wife   So let him come.

Señorita (*crying out from offstage*)   Esperancita . . . Esperancita's dead.

Perico (*struggling to his feet*)   You have poisoned death itself, Maria. (*He tears off his tie.*) I am alone. This place is a grave. A bottomless pit. A trap. (*Pause. Then crying out.*) Maria, Maria. Don't try to stop me. I shall devour your mulato children because you can cause such fire in the blood. Maria, Maria. (*Going out.*) If there is any justice, God will have no need to forgive me.

The characters of the **Chorus** *begin to move. They move their hands and bodies as if they were filling in a hole. The beating of a drum.*

Scene Nine

Chorus
    The man is dead, the man is dead.
    Cover him with earth,
    Throw earth on his head.

Maria *enters suddenly.*

Scene Ten

Maria   I have won the contest. I am going for the mirror, Perico Piedra Fina. It only remains for Julián to return. (*Cruel laugh.*) Madness or death. (*The laugh becomes a terrible, implacable cry.*)

Act Three

Scene One

Early hours of the morning. A reddish glow envelops the scene. At intervals a distant tom-tom is heard. **Madam Pitonisa** *and* **Doctor Mandinga** *enter cautiously stage-left. She presses a straw basket against her stomach. She is dressed in white with lots of necklaces and bracelets. She is small, fat, broad-shouldered. She contrasts markedly with her companion who is tall and heavily built. Under his arm he has a packet of herbs wrapped in newspaper. He wears a grey suit, which is frayed and dirty. Both* **Madam Pitonisa** *and* **Doctor Mandinga** *are old and black.*

Pitonisa   This has to be decided.

Doctor   Are you sure?

Pitonisa   Of course I am.

Doctor   How do you know?

Pitonisa   I can smell it in the air.

Doctor (*stammering, looking around*)   It's a very ugly thing. (*Looks at her maliciously.*) You old rascal. (*Laughing.*) No one can get one over on you.

Pitonisa (*whispering*)   Be quiet! Don't speak so loud! (*Change of tone.*) You know I'm always right.

Doctor (*a little louder*)   If it's proof you need, just ask me.

Pitonisa   Then why such agitation?

Doctor   Do you think she'll come?

Pitonisa (*whispering, with a sense of great mystery*)   Who?

Doctor (*imitating her tone of voice*)   Maria.

Pitonisa (*quickly, preparing to go off*)   Careful.

Doctor (*with a certain clumsiness, as if taken by surprise*)   Who do you think is listening?

Pitonisa (*agitated, whispering*)   Let's go over here! (**Doctor Mandinga** *runs after her on tiptoe.*) What a simpleton you are!

They hide. Pause.

Doctor (*sticking his head out from their hiding place*)   They almost caught me in fraganti . . .

Pitonisa (*emerging from their hiding place*)   Who was it?

Doctor (*emerging*)   I've no idea.

Pitonisa (*making signs in the air*)   By the nine devils, by the bones of all the dead . . . and the heavenly trumpet . . .

Doctor   Is anything the matter?

Pitonisa (*looking around all parts of the stage*)   No, nothing. (*Change of tone.*) I felt a blast of cold air. Something terrible is approaching . . . If it is Erundina . . . I can't stand the sight of her . . . Keep your eyes open over there.

Doctor   Do you think that she'd do that to him?

Pitonisa   Who, man, who?

Doctor   Maria.

Pitonisa   Do you think that she can stop herself? (*Smiling.*)

Doctor   She is strong.

Pitonisa   But if I oppose her, she will end up doing what I say.

Doctor   First of all you have to know what happened exactly.

Pitonisa   No need to find out. We know what happened. It was meant to be. (*Looking in all directions.*) There is blood in every corner. (*She smiles. Pause.*) She has to get to the end beyond the end of things.

Doctor   Things are going badly.

Pitonisa   Yesterday I showed her the cards.

Doctor   There is blood. (*He moves downstage.*)

Pitonisa   She needs to screw up her courage. Next I shall show her the snails. Already it makes my hair stand on end . . . (*Tenderly.*) We have to help her, Doctor Mandinga. (*Downstage.*) This is very serious. Come out of there. I know you, Eleutorio. Come out here. There's no one about to catch us unawares. (*With a great effort she places the basket on the ground.*) These rheumatics, you know, are going to finish me off one day.

Doctor (*awkwardly*)   I would have helped you if you'd asked.

Pitonisa   It doesn't matter. (*Rummaging in the basket.*) I'm going to sprinkle the powders. (*She can't find what she wants.*) I can't think where I've put them. Did I give them to you? One of these days I'll lose my head for sure. (*Still looking.*) Keep yourself calm, Madam Pitonisa. You worry about the silliest things. Now, did I bring them or not? (*Pause. Gesturing.*) The most important thing of all and I go and forget it.

Doctor   Look properly, Madam.

Pitonisa   What do you think I am doing, man? Are you sure you haven't got them yourself? (**Doctor Mandinga** *shows no reaction.*) Ah, here they are. (*Pause. She opens the box and smells it. Change of tone.*) We'd better hurry, make a start. Sprinkle some basil and rosemary. (**Doctor Mandinga** *takes some twigs from the packet and begins to sprinkle them, as if blessing the stage.*) To the powers of darkness . . . (**Madam Pitonisa** *sprinkles the powders over the stage.*) Through the evil of this world, this hell, suffering, purification . . . Through the evil of this world . . . Through the evil of this hell . . . Through the evil of this world, this hell, suffering, purification. (*She stops centre stage, turns on herself twice.* **Doctor Mandinga** *is towards the back of the stage, blowing and making unintelligible sounds.*) Appear, spirit that purifies . . . (*She turns on herself. In a trance.*) In the name of the nine devils . . . (**Doctor Mandinga** *stamps three times on the ground.*) In the

name of the nine devils at every window. In the name of the
nine devils at every door. In the name of the nine devils who
confuse our thoughts. O spirit that purifies, do your work.
Do your work both here and in the hereafter.

Pause. Slowly the lighting grows less intense. **Madame Pitonisa**
and **Doctor Mandinga** *leave stage-left.*

Scene Two

Maria *enters. Her face and her movements reflect her unease and
anguish.*

Maria (*searching*)   Is anyone there? (*Pause.*) No one,
nothing. Will I at last be able to . . . ? If there was only
someone . . . (*Muttering.*) This is a closed circle. (*She comes
downstage a little.*) Julián, Julián . . . (*Change of tone. Weakly.*)
Tonight seems endless, as if time, the hours, the minutes
and I myself did not exist . . . as if we were a dark and
bottomless pit . . . O red night, redder than the blood that
has stained this place . . . and I am here, waiting, waiting,
but waiting for who? Of course I know that he won't come.
My hopes are all in vain. Why should he come if all my
words mean nothing, if all my tears . . . (*She sobs.*) What am I
to do? What shall I do? (*She kneels, then sits. She weeps.*) I have
tried everything. I have tried the impossible, and the
impossible has failed me . . .

Scene Three

Pitonisa (*entering imperiously with* **Doctor Mandinga**)   Not
so much weeping.

Maria (*taken aback*)   Why are you here?

Pitonisa   Because you need me?

Maria   How do you know? Who told you?

Pitonisa   For me to know what's going on, no one has to tell me. Don't you believe me? Don't you have faith? Pity the person who has no faith. (*Pause.*) You have to get . . .

Maria (*almost muttering*) . . . to the end beyond the end of things. (*Weeping, desperate.*) Oh, Madam Pitonisa, Madam . . . (*She bends forward towards* **Madam Pitonisa**.)

Pitonisa (*importantly*)   Help is at hand.

Madam Pitonisa *sits on a step above* **Maria**. **Maria** *rests her head on* **Madam**'s *knees.*

Doctor   It is so dark!

Pitonisa   Stop crying now. Raise you head up.

Doctor (*making a sign in the air.*)   Some light for this poor woman!

Maria (*weeping*)   He hasn't come. I thought he would appear there, between the sheets, angry, insulting me, ready to do his worst, but close, so close to me . . . I've made such efforts.

Doctor (*opens the packet of herbs and begins to wave it in the air*) Between heaven and earth . . .

Doctor Mandiga *sweeps the ground towards the door at the back.*

Maria   If he dragged me on the ground, if he made me kiss the dust, the walls, the stones, I'd willingly do it. I'd give my blood to see him, to know what he's thinking, to know if he still feels something, however small . . .

Pitonisa   You must stop this. Calm yourself.

Maria   Standing there, naked, looking at me angrily, squeezing my throat, throwing me aside, humiliating me . . . It wouldn't matter. Because it's him. Just think of how I've suffered.

Doctor (*kneeling, hitting the ground three times with his hand*)   I call upon the powers of hell . . .

Pitonisa (*to* **Maria**, *feigning compassion*)   Of course, Maria. (*Change of tone.*) You are a child. And all I've done to try to help you!

Maria   I'm not complaining. I'm only complaining of him, of Julián . . . He's always thought that I am worthless . . . and he's told me so . . . time and time again. And that's what always drives me crazy . . . and I shout at him and scream at him and tell him I never want to see him again, and he says that's OK, and he acts as if nothing at all had happened. But I go back, although I've said a thousand times I wouldn't, and I look for him and plead with him and tell him that he was right and I was a fool, and that he's a thousand times better than me. And this time it's so much worse, Madam.

Pitonisa (*with great tenderness*)   You went down the wrong road, Maria.

Doctor (*chanting*)   In the name of fear . . . nightmare . . . Beelzebub.

Maria (*evoking the past, obsessed*)   He came to me that night. I'd told him not to, that what he wanted wasn't possible, that circumstances were against it, that Erundina had said no, that it was madness, that Father was sick, that I would call out, that my brother was in the next room, that he ought to leave me alone . . . But he paid no attention, I couldn't resist, his words ensnared me . . . I heard sounds, I heard music, I protested . . . (*Pause. Overcome.*) I let him in . . .

Pitonisa (*feigning compassion*)   The years pass and still you are just the same.

Doctor (*invoking*)   By those who are hanged, condemned, betrayed . . .

Simultaneously.

Maria (*to* **Pitonisa**)
My brother advised me from the beginning. He could see what was coming . . . and father and Erundina and Salustiano . . .

Pitonisa (*quickly, interrupting*)
Are you telling me that . . . ?

Maria (*quickly, interrupting*)
Oh, no, Madam. I'm very grateful to you. But I . . .

Pitonisa (*very dry*)
Accept the situation as it is.

Doctor (*an invocation*)
By red-hot irons, cauldrons of boiling oil, the tombs that open, the dead that rise, the horror that goes on, suffering, death and war. In the name of fear and nightmare and Beelzebub. (*Crying out.*) Light and progress for the soul in anguish.

Maria (*desperate*)   No, not that. I can't accept it. I can't forget. That would be too easy. I would never do such a thing. Do you think my life has been some childish game? Do you think that what I have suffered, my dreams, my sleepless nights, can all be forgotten, as if nothing at all had happened? I refuse to accept it. Do you hear me? I refuse. Do you think forgetting would be enough? Who could erase my children from my mind? They are here: calling, pleading and crying out. It is something that has to be faced. (*Pause. She takes a few steps downstage. For a moment she becomes sweet and calm.*) Each time I see them, I see Julián. They are Julián. It's not only I who need him. They need him too. Julián is our destiny.

Pitonisa (*laughing mockingly*)   But what are you saying, Maria? You can't be serious. Of course you can't. You are having a laugh at my expense. (*Laughing loudly.*) If it's the truth, I can't believe it.

Maria (*with a certain bitterness*)   Then you'd better believe it. I am not myself. I am someone else. My thoughts, my joys, my despair, even my crimes, everything of mine is Julián. My life has no other meaning.

Pitonisa (*with great pity*)   You see, you've hit the nail right on the head. Can't you see all that is false, has little to do with reality? Just stop to think of what you are doing, saying, hiding, of what goes on around you, of everything Julián says and does. Can't you see it's a mistake? What are you tying to defend? Tell me what you think: that you have Julián? Have you ever had him? It's always been the same as now . . . (*Short pause. Deliberately.*) And what is your part in this? (*Short pause.*) Is it your fate to be living in this void, hanging on his every wish, on all his meanness of spirit, on 'will he come?', or 'who is he with?', and never knowing anything? Is that to be your fate?

Maria (*furiously*)   Go away, leave me alone! You are just the same as Erundina. Just the same as the rest of them. They all tell me the same thing. Why can't you leave me in peace? Do you think I can't find a way out? Do you think I can't sort things out as I did before? (*With sarcasm.*) I didn't know that everyone was so concerned with my well-being. What does it matter to them? Just because I have spoken of my pain and my fears, does everyone think that I'm asking for protection?

Madam Pitonisa *and* **Doctor Mandinga**, *down-stage, begin to circle round and to mumble rhythmically, as in a chant, together or separately.*

Pitonisa   Great Lucifer, lord and master of all rebellious spirits, I pray be favourable towards this request . . .

Doctor   O Prince Beelzebub, protect me in this enterprise . . .

Pitonisa   O count Astaroth, favour me tonight . . .

Doctor   Leave your dwelling. Wherever you may be, come and speak to me . . .

Pitonisa   Grant strength and will . . .

Maria (*like a fury*)   Don't think it will be so easy. Don't think that they can defeat me.

Pitonisa (*pityingly*)   Maria . . .

Doctor (*copying her*)   Maria . . .

Maria (*like a cornered animal*)   I am not Maria. I am not anyone. I am not anything. I am myself.

Maria *has suddenly fallen into a trance.* **Madame Pitonisa** *and* **Doctor Mandinga** proceed with their invocations. They circle, as if they were heavenly bodies, moving in opposite directions from the front to the back of the stage.

Pitonisa   On the contrary, I shall oblige you through the power of Alpha and Omega . . .

Doctor   And the angels of light, Adonai, Elohim and Jehovah. You shall obey.

Pitonisa   Obey at once.

Doctor   Or you will be in torment for ever.

Maria, *in a trance, walks around the stage as she converses with* **Julián**'s *secret demons.*

Maria (*anxiously*)   Julián! (*Her face lights up.*) Oh, Julián! (*As if* **Julián** *were hitting her.*) What are you doing? Are you mad? Why? Why? . . . (*Choking on her sobs.*) No, no. Stop. Wait. Please! (*As if she were offering him money.*) Here, take it! It's yours. All of it. Yes, yes. I want nothing for myself. I'm a good woman. You know I'm always good to you. Perico Piedra Fina is plotting something against me, I know he is. But you love me, isn't that true? I know you don't care if my father's sick and dying, or that my brother went to prison for a robbery he didn't commit. It was me, Julián, me . . . I did it for you . . . Don't laugh . . . (*Trying to convince him.*) You're a man, you have to make the decision, and because you aren't like other men . . . (*Passionately.*) I need you. I can't be here alone . . . Don't leave me. You can do what you want and I'll follow you . . . I'll obey. This world is pointless if you aren't there. I will be your shadow, anything you want.

Long pause. She stops. She has suddenly seen her terrible, nightmarish past. **Madam Pitonisa** *and* **Doctor Mandinga** *are upstage, like two phantoms. She speaks with great intensity.*

You have left me for ever. (*Pause.*) But I shall take revenge. The only thing that is left to me. Madame Pitonisa, I begin to see it all. (**Madam Pitonisa** *doesn't move.*) You were right all the time. Julián is not my destiny. Where is the mirror? (*Shouting.*) Erundina. Erundina! (*Beginning to recognise herself in the mirror.*) I have a body. There it is. That is how I look. (*She laughs bitterly.*) My body is the mirror. (*Beginning to laugh.*) The mirror. It tells me what I have to do. 'Don't be afraid. Be confident. Life, your life, is the only thing you have, the only valuable thing.' How have you been so blind so long? Perhaps this is all a deception. No, no! (*Her laughter has a ring of madness.*) What a fool, what a fool I am . . . If you only knew, Julián . . . if you only knew I no longer want you, you are nothing to me now. (*Laughing crazily.*)

Pause. **Maria**, *downstage, falls to her knees.* **Madam Pitonisa** *brings a large knife with a black handle. She approaches* **Maria** *from the left.* **Doctor Mandinga** *brings a small wax doll. He approaches* **Maria** *from the right.*

Pitonisa (*to* **Maria**, *whispering*)   Here it is. (*She gives* **Maria** *the knife.*)

Doctor (*to* **Maria**, *whispering*)   Pierce it now! (*He gives* **Maria** *the doll.*)

Maria (*staring at the knife and the doll*)   No, not now.

Pitonisa   You have to do it.

Doctor   Don't lose this opportunity.

Pitonisa   Speak the familiar words.

Doctor   So that he disappears.

Pitonisa   Be strong.

Doctor   Be forceful.

Pitonisa   Say it at once and once and for all. (*She commences an invocation.*) O spirit from hell . . . (*She goes out.*)

Maria (*repeating the invocation weakly*)   O spirit from hell. I beg you put your powers at my service, in order to torment him and make him disappear . . .

Maria, *the wax doll and the knife fall to the ground.*

Scene Four

Erundina *and* **Señorita Amparo**.

Erundina   At least they've gone to sleep.

Amparo   I feel I am to blame. When they started to shout 'We want Mamá', I didn't know what to say.

Erundina   Be quiet. Don't torment me.

Amparo   Did she speak? Did she tell you what to do? What did she say?

Erundina   She said nothing. She did nothing.

Amparo   We should have stayed . . .

Erundina   It's better this way.

Amparo   But it's our duty. We could have stopped her.

Erundina   Who can stop the wind or fire when they are out of control?

Amparo   You're right . . . (*Pause.*) Look, there she is!

Erundina   Let's go. We have to let her get on with it.

Amparo   We ought to tell her the children want her.

Erundina   Much better not to. She has to sort things out for herself. She has to find herself.

They both go out.

Scene Five

Maria *alone.*

Maria (*desperately*)   I can't, I can't. (*Pause.*) But I have to do
it. (*She takes a deep breath.*) I have to do it, Madam Pitonisa. I
have to do it, Erundina. I have to do it, Doctor Mandinga. I
have to do it, my children. (*Pause.*) I need to do it. I need to
rise up against the Maria who drags me back and shames
me. (*She rises.*) I know it's not the other's fault. It's you,
Maria, you who are pushing me into the void. You are my
enemy. I am the other form of myself, the one that is in the
mirror, the one who was waiting, who was afraid to appear,
who couldn't see she was alone; alone, though she didn't
want to be, although she believed she could not bear such
loneliness. (*Forcefully.*) Leave me! Now I understand. Now I
begin to discover what surrounds me, what belonged to me
and I dismissed. Now I have no fear. I know I am groping in
the darkness; but this is my path and I have no fear. Now I
know that love is as strong as life and death, and that life,
death and love are maybe the same thing. Now I know what
I am. (*Short hysterical laugh.*) What I am, and nothing holds
me back, neither fear nor humiliation, and, knowing that, I
am myself. Good and bad mean nothing to me now; I have
put all that behind me. Now I am my true self. Your arms,
Julián, your body, Julián, are in the past. And I, who have
so far clung to a dream, am in need of life, of life itself:
horror, blood, tenderness, indifference, crime. I know I am
in need of life, that this body of mine that was dead and is
now Maria, myself, is pushing me towards life. (*Pause.
Suddenly absent.*) Where are my children? (*Shouting.*) Erundina.
(*Pause. Another cry.*) Señorita Amparo. (*Pause.*) Where have
they gone? (*Pause. With hate, but calmly.*) Julián, I shall avenge
myself. You won't be able to stop me. I have murdered
those I thought would block my path . . . It will be what you
cannot imagine. I shall get to the end beyond the end of
things. (*Shouting.*) My children. Where are my children?
(*Pause. Change of tone.*) Now it is not love; or perhaps it is; a
love that goes beyond you, beyond me, beyond words; a

love that calls for sacrifice and hate; a love that destroys everything in order to begin again. (*Long pause.*) Be quiet. Here are my children. Let no one wake them. Julián is dead and they will continue to sleep for ever. (*A gesture to impose silence.*) My life begins, Julián. Children, my life begins. Maria has found herself. (*As if a multitude of mirrors had appeared on stage.*) A mirror here, a mirror there. Another here, another there. I am surrounded. I have become a mirror myself. (*She laughs. Pause.*) Be quiet . . . there is so much blood. Blood. Blood. (*Suddenly afraid.*) I am drowning in blood . . . I am drowning in this blood. (*A fearful cry.*) Who can stop this blood?

Maria *falls to her knees, her back to the audience.*

Scene Six

The **Barber** *and the* **Boy** *enter stage left.* **Antonio's Wife** *and the* **Bongoman** *enter stage-right.* **Maria** *is centre stage.*

Wife (*looking in all directions*)   Has anyone seen Maria?

Boy (*to the audience*)   Has anyone seen Maria?

Wife   Someone has to advise her.

Boy   People are giving evidence. Black days will come, blacker than we have ever known.

Barber   Don't speak of what we have known.

Wife   It doesn't count. Does it matter that Maria has struggled so hard? It doesn't matter one little bit.

Boy   The only thing to do is shout.

Barber   Shout, shout, that's the truth.

Wife (*shouthing*)   Where are you, Maria?

Barber   We are all riding the same horse.

Bongoman   Riding, no; we are all drowning!

Barber   Don't bring about another misfortune.

Boy   We have to stop Maria.

Wife   Maria, please turn back.

Boy   Control yourself.

Barber   Come down from that cloud.

Bongoman   Violence is a double-edged sword.

Wife   Be careful.

Barber   Think.

Boy   You have two children.

Bongoman   Two sons, they are your future.

Wife   You have to sacrifice.

Barber   Bring them up.

Wife   Let them learn to survive in the world.

Bongoman   As parents have done from time immemorial.

Wife   Avoid this crime.

Barber   Do not become a murderess.

Boy   Do not defile your blood.

Bongoman   Do not let passion blind you.

Wife (*dramatically*)   Stop. (*In a solemn tone.*) Do not repeat the history of Cuca Miraflores, the beloved wife of Colonel Pancho Pujilato . . . (*In a gossipy tone.*) Antonio told me how that poor woman, many years ago, although it seems just yesterday, set fire to her house while her children slept, and threw herself into the sea.

Bongoman   A sea of blood around us.

Barber   What can we do?

Woman   Blood, blood that's cursed . . .

Boy (*shouting*)   Maria, Maria . . .

Bongoman   She did us a favour, ridding us of Perico Piedra Fina, of his shadow, of his stick.

Wife   Oh, Maria, we are in your debt . . .

Barber   When the police make their inquires, we'll tell them it was an accident.

Chorus (*recognising* **Maria**)   Maria, don't drown yourself in blood.

Scene Seven

Maria (*getting up and picking up the knife*)   Blood is a mirror that saves me.

Child's voice (*off, crying*)   Mamá, Mamá.

Second Child's voice   Mamá, Mamá.

Maria (*going out majestically*)   Don't be afraid, my children. Soon you shall sleep. My children shall sleep soon. My children shall sleep soon.

Chorus (*solemnly, almost singing*)
  Blood, blood, blood, blood.
  Don't drown yourself in so much blood.
  Blood, blood, blood, blood.
  Don't drown yourself in so much blood.
  Blood, blood, blood, blood.
  Oh, blood. She drowns herself in blood.

The characters of the **Chorus** *fall on their knees.*

Scene Eight

Maria *enters with bloodstained hands.* **Julián** *enters stage left, his expression wild.*

Julián (*gesturing furiously*)   So here you are! Congratulations! (*Observing her from head to foot.*) Who would have thought it? Maria, Maria the little angel. And all the time she was a devil. (**Maria** *is silent.*) Come on now, stop trying to play the fool. (**Maria** *is silent.*) You drive me too far and I'll break you in pieces. (**Maria** *is silent.*) You know that I always do what I want. (*Beating his chest.*) I do everything like a man. (**Maria** *is silent.*) Oh, no. I'm not going to hit you. But do you think that I don't know what you were trying to do? Do you take me for a fool? (**Maria** *is silent.*) Look at me! Do you think I'm a child who sucks its finger? You poisoned the old man with the wine . . . and then his daughter fell for it too, suspecting nothing. (**Maria** *is silent.*) You wanted to kill me, right? But you missed the target. Be careful what you say. Everyone is talking about what you've done. The police will be here . . . let's see you try to get out of that . . . I'm finished with that sort of people. (**Maria** *is silent.*) I've come for my children. I intend to take them far away from here . . . where this place will be an almost forgotten memory. (**Maria** *is silent.*) So tell me where they are. I'll have them one way or another. (*He goes out. Silence. A loud cry, off.*) Maria, what have you done? What have you done?

The sound of a drumbeat. The characters of the **Chorus** *rise to the sound of the music and encircle* **Maria**, *who tries to escape.*

Chorus (*chanting furiously*)   Murderer, murderer, murderer.

The **Chorus** *commence a desperate struggle with* **Maria**. *She defends herself. One after another, they try to overcome her. She struggles frantically.*

Maria (*panting. She utters a wild cry*)   I am God.

Maria *is overcome. The* **Chorus** *drag her downstage. Then, horrified, they raise her on high like a trophy.*